Bon Appetit !

The MAVERICK COOKBOOK

The MAVERICK COOKBOOK

ICONIC RECIPES & TALES FROM NEW MEXICO

LYNN CLINE

RECIPE PHOTOGRAPHS BY
GUY AMBROSINO

LeafStormPress

SANTA FE, NEW MEXICO

CONTENTS

A NOTE FROM THE AUTHOR

THE IDEA FOR *THE MAVERICK COOKBOOK* CAME TO ME OVER THE YEARS AS I THOUGHT about the many fascinating people who, across the ages, have shaped New Mexico cuisine. Starting with the early Puebloan people who grew beans, corn and squash, the list is long and varied. It encompasses eras of Spanish settlement, the Santa Fe Trail, the railroads, the artists' and writers' colonies, the Manhattan Project, as well as the arrival of gourmet dining and the contemporary Farm To Table movement.

The 12 mavericks chosen here represent the spirit of their times, and of their place—New Mexico. They embody unique and fiery passions, and their food reflects this—food that sustained them in their important work. It is simple food that honors the garden, food to be eaten alone or with family and friends. Some of it is celebratory. Some of it is pure comfort. All of it is inspired by the lives of these 12 extraordinary people who called New Mexico home, at least for a while.

This list of mavericks is by no means complete, as countless others have made significant contributions to New Mexico cuisine. But it represents the many risk-takers who have sought out robust lives in New Mexico, and who have stirred the pot.

The stories and recipes herein rest squarely on the shoulders of previous books that served as rich source material. Inspired by the history of each era, most of the scenes described are fictional imaginings of a day or a moment in the life of one of these mavericks. Each original recipe reflects its era as well, with authentic ingredients and traditional techniques popular at the time. Most are intentionally simple, made with readily available ingredients.

As you journey through the pages, I hope you'll savor the stories of these New Mexico legends, and be inspired to make the recipes in your own kitchen so you can enjoy the food that reflects the celebrated and beloved cuisine of the Southwest.

CHAPTER ONE

PUEBLO GRANDMOTHER (1350s)

Hold on to what is good,
Even if it's a handful of earth.
Hold on to what you believe,
Even if it's a tree that stands by itself.
Hold on to what you must do,
Even if it's a long way from here.
Hold on to your life,
Even if it's easier to let go.
Hold on to my hand,
Even if someday I'll be gone away from you.

~ PUEBLO INDIAN PRAYER

THE SETTING SUN RESTS ON THE EDGE OF THE SKY, AND GRANDMOTHER IS IN THE kitchen preparing the last meal of the day. Clothed in a buckskin wrap she embroidered with colorful porcupine quill and wearing bracelets and necklaces of turquoise and white shells, she moves swiftly around the small room in preparation for the arrival of her daughter's family. The cooking fire crackles in the dark kitchen.

She stirs a clay bowl filled with batter for the corncakes and heats a stone slab over the fire where she'll cook them. Then she stirs a small, soot-covered clay pot propped against a rock so it stands upright in the cooking fire. This pot is full of venison stewing with corn, beans, roots and herbs for seasoning. She's also made some dried yucca preserve, a sweet treat for the children.

The walls of the small room are whitewashed with burnt gypsum. The doorways are covered with deer hides and robes to keep in the heat. A plaited yucca leaf mat stands in one corner. The only other room is for sleeping.

Surrounding Grandmother are water jars, bean pots and other clay vessels she's made. Some she's painted with figures, others with symbols for lightning, clouds, rain. Her favorite vessel—one she made with her daughter when she was young—is a simple earthen bowl, painted white with black figures. Grandmother learned to make pottery from her mother as a child, in the same way she taught her daughter the tradition. And now her granddaughter is just beginning to make pots.

These vessels are used for storing and cooking food—the corn, beans and squash that make up the foundation of their diet. They grow well together in the ground, up on the mesa. The corn grows tall, providing shade and shelter for the beans and squash. Together, the three provide a healthy diet.

She uses a flat stone slab for grinding the corn, and crushes it on a plate made of hardened lava. She dried the corn weeks ago, in preparation for winter. It will be used in stews and other dishes, including her grandson's favorite—piñon blue corncakes.

Grandmother has soaked the beans and left them cooking in large bean pots. Tonight, they will eat the end-of-the-summer squash—lighter and sweeter than the winter squash—a treat with its delicious edible flowers. Later, as the winds grow cold, Grandmother will place a whole winter squash in the fire coals. When it softens, she will split it open and scoop out the flesh to use in soups and stews. And she will roast the seeds—delicious!—or press them to extract their oil.

What a blessing, this beautiful Earth! And the elk, deer, antelope and rabbit that run upon it. The river and its fish. The ceaselessly gobbling turkeys. The juniper and piñon trees, and their flavorful nuts. The seeds of the amaranth. The yucca and cholla and their fruits. The berries and wild honey. All the green and silver grasses.

The food is almost ready for tonight's meal. Grandmother steps outside to look up at the rising Harvest Moon and offers a silent prayer for rain. It's been a dry season and people are worried there will be no vegetables to eat during the winter. If the rainclouds don't come soon, they'll have to break into their stored foods. Still, they have corn, along with beans and squash. And tonight's dark sky is a beautiful sight, streaked with orange and blues as the last ray of sun slips away.

She thinks of how life revolves around the seasons, from the annual Corn Dance to the Deer Hunt, held every winter and spring. Soon, when the moon is new in this early autumn season, the great Rabbit Hunt will take place, a tradition that brings the whole village together for days of feasting and merriment.

Tonight, the air is warm and the village is alive with the sounds of laughter and singing. But later, when it quiets down, she will hear the rushing of the river and the howls of coyotes and wolves. For now, it's time to go inside and prepare the corncakes.

Long ago, when she was younger than her daughter is now, corncakes carried an important message for her. The man who would become her husband, the man who would share dinner with her for so many years, had begun to court her. So, Grandmother had happily filled a jar with corncakes and a sweet yucca paste made from the fruit, carried it to his house and placed it in front of him as a sign that she accepted his offer of marriage.

Although he left this world a few years ago, Grandfather's spirit lives on in their grandchildren, who, she realizes, should be here soon. She places a stack of corncakes on the floor, next to the pot with the venison stew, and with that, the table is spread. They will eat seated on the floor around the fire as it casts long shadows around the room.

She feels her hunger and her longing for family around her. Then in a rush from outside, she hears the sound of her grandchildren's laughter approaching the doorway. And then, there is her daughter, stepping into the room, asking if she might help.

The family gathers around, finding places to sit on the floor. Everyone is hungry. But first they must offer prayers and thanks to the animals for their sacrifice. Grandmother sprinkles cornmeal to the four directions—North, South, East and West—then tosses some in the air and on the ground before her as thanks for the food they've gathered from surrounding forests. "It is well," she says, looking into the eyes of each of her family members. And she knows that it is good. A blessed life.

"*Hoya*," she smiles. "Let's eat."

BLUE CORN ATOLE

SERVES 4

Atole was a staple for the Pueblo Indians, who relied heavily on corn for their diet. In this recipe, it has the consistency of Cream of Wheat and a nutty, earthy flavor. You can top it with many ingredients, from nuts and syrup to honey, grated cheese and cinnamon and butter.

2 cups cold water
1 cup blue cornmeal
2 tablespoons lard
½ teaspoon salt
¼ cup pecans, chopped, for topping
¼ cup honey, molasses or other sweetener

Stir 2 cups cold water into the blue cornmeal in a medium bowl and set aside to let the mixture dissolve.

In a large pot, boil 2 cups of water, and then stir in the lard and salt. Continue stirring over medium heat and slowly add the cornmeal slurry, stirring until it thickens. Remove from heat. Sprinkle pecans on top and serve with honey, molasses or other sweetener.

ANCESTRAL PUEBLO PEOPLE

From 1150 to 1550 CE (Common Era), the site known today as Bandelier National Monument was a thriving village where many clans lived together, farming the mesa tops, hunting deer and other animals for meat and skins, fishing the rivers and streams and harvesting the forests. They followed the cycles of the seasons with rituals and traditions that continue today in New Mexican's 19 pueblos.

The Bandelier people were ancestors of the Pueblo people, and the Santa Fe area once served as the ancient capital of the Pueblo Indian kingdom. Ruins of ancient villages have been found all around the city. Remnants of other great Pueblo settlements that existed during this same time have been found in New Mexico at Pecos National Historic Park and Chaco Canyon; in Arizona at Canyon de Chelly; and in Colorado at Mesa Verde.

PIÑON BLUE CORNCAKES

MAKES 12-14 PANCAKES

Blue corn grows in a range of colors from a pale blue to a dark purple, and has more nutritional value than other types of corn. Its delicate sweetness pairs well with apricots and piñon nuts.

1 cup blue cornmeal
2 tablespoons Vanilla Sugar (see Kitchen Clue)
1 tablespoon baking powder
¼ teaspoon salt
2 eggs, lightly beaten
1 cup milk
3 tablespoons butter, melted
A few tablespoons butter, for cooking
¼ cup piñon nuts

In a large mixing bowl, combine the blue cornmeal with Vanilla Sugar, baking powder and salt.

Beat the eggs in a separate bowl then stir in the milk and melted butter. Add the wet ingredients to the dry ingredients, stirring swiftly.

Preheat the oven to 250 degrees.

Melt a tablespoon of butter on a griddle or in a large pan over medium heat. Drop the batter from the tip of a spoon to form each pancake and sprinkle a few piñon nuts on top. Cook the pancakes for a few minutes on one side, until bubbles form on the top, then flip and cook a few minutes more on the other side. Keep the finished pancakes warm in the oven. Serve with maple syrup, fruit preserves or Spiced Apricots.

KITCHEN CLUE

Vanilla Sugar is easy to make and lends a wonderful flavor to pies, cakes, cookies and even coffee. Slice a vanilla bean lengthwise in half and scrape the interior into 2 cups of sugar. Mix with your hands until the scrapings break up a bit. Bury the bean in the sugar and store in an airtight container for 1 to 2 weeks before removing the bean. Keep stored in the airtight container.

MICACEOUS CLAY-COOKED BEANS

SERVES 4-6

If you don't have a micaceous clay bean pot, you can use a covered, oven-proof ceramic or glass baking dish for this traditional dish, flavored with the ingredients of ancient New Mexico. For a vegetarian version, simply omit the bacon.

2½ cups (one pound) dried pinto beans, rinsed and picked over
1 medium onion, coarsely chopped
5 big cloves garlic, minced
1 tablespoon olive oil
3 strips bacon, diced
1 teaspoon epazote leaves, dried and crumbled
1 tablespoon chile powder, preferably Chimayó (see Kitchen Clue)
1 bay leaf, whole
½ teaspoon cumin powder
5-6 cups water
1 teaspoon salt
1 teaspoon freshly ground black pepper

Soak the beans in cold water for 8-12 hours or overnight. Drain.

Combine all of the ingredients in the bean pot or baking dish and place on the lower rack of an unheated oven. Set the heat to 400 degrees and cook the beans for 1½ hours, adding the salt after the first hour of cooking.

Remove the pot from oven and stir, adjusting the seasonings if necessary. Reduce the temperature to 375 degrees and cook until the beans are soft, about 40 minutes. Remove from the oven, let sit, covered, for 10 minutes and serve.

ROASTED ACORN SQUASH

SERVES 4

A simple Pueblo autumn dish, traditionally cooked in the coals of a fire. This modern version includes a sprinkling of sage and the sweetness of maple syrup.

2 large acorn squash
1-2 tablespoons olive oil
2 tablespoons butter
2 tablespoons maple syrup
2-3 tablespoons fresh sage, chopped
¼ teaspoon salt
¼ teaspoon freshly ground black pepper

Preheat oven to 350 degrees.

Cut squash in half lengthwise and scoop out the seeds. Rub the outer skin with the olive oil. Place on a baking pan, cut sides down, and roast until tender when pierced with a fork, about 30-45 minutes. Flip the squash over and dot the cavities with butter, drizzle with the maple syrup and sprinkle with the sage, salt and pepper. Return to the oven and bake for an additional 5 minutes, or until the butter is bubbling but not yet browned.

KITCHEN CLUE

In New Mexico, **chile and chili** are two very different foods. *Chile* refers to hot peppers or the pepper plant, while *chili* refers to a hearty dish made with beef, hot peppers or chile powder and usually beans (sometimes called *chili con carne*). But the rest of the country uses chili to mean both the fruit and the beef dish, confusing everyone who visits New Mexico. There's even a third spelling, *chilli*, mostly used by the British.

The word *chile/chili* evolved from the Aztec word *chil* (pepper). The Spanish added the "e," and it was Spanish Conquistador Don Juan de Oñate who brought the green chile pepper into the region in 1598. The chile grown in New Mexico is noteworthy, from the earthy, sweet green chile grown in Hatch (in southern New Mexico), to the Chimayó red chile, which has a rich, complex flavor with bright citrus notes and is grown north of Santa Fe in the tiny village of Chimayó.

However you spell it, the fabled chile of New Mexico is delicious and a star ingredient in Southwestern cuisine. Try adding Chimayó red chile powder to your dishes instead of the regular "chili powder" from the spice section of your grocery store and you won't believe the difference. It's easy to find and order online.

CHAPTER TWO

DOÑA TULES, QUEEN OF CARDS

(1840s)

"It was a time when all lived dangerously,
and Doña Tules Barcélo more dangerously than all."

RUTH LAUGHLIN

THE GREEN-EYED, RED-HAIRED BEAUTY SITS AT A TABLE IN THE BACK OF BARCÉLO Palace saloon, dealing monte, her fingers wrapped in rings, her neck draped with heavy gold chains. Her eyes reveal nothing. She knows the game, she knows the men around the card table are lonesome and she knows, too, that many of them come simply to stare at her lovely features. She is wise—and a shrewd business-woman—and she knows how to capitalize around the gambling table.

Her opulent gambling saloon on Santa Fe's bustling Palace Avenue is jeweled with glittering crystal chandeliers, fine European carpets, red velvet curtains, etched glass mirrors and imported European furniture brought to this remote town by wagon trains on the Santa Fe Trail. Elegant mirrors stretch from white marble shelves to the rafters. The room is filled with carved *trasteros* (dish cupboards), tables, chairs and one great chandelier in the middle, casting the brilliance of a hundred candles. There's a cantina and a wooden dance floor, where a live orchestra plays from a high platform. Perched in a tall seat nearby, the spotter watches for card cheats and fights.

How far she has come, this transplant from Sonora, Mexico, where she was born Maria Gertrudis Barcélo at the turn of the century. Her family moved to the territory of New Mexico, traveling up El Camino Real, or the Royal Road, after Mexico won its independence from Spain in 1821. Since then, she's led a tumultuous life, surviving a Navajo attack in Taos, losing two children in infancy and becoming a widow. Yet today, she's one of the wealthiest and most powerful people in Santa Fe, reigning over the region's most infamous saloon.

Doña Tules turns her gaze down to shuffle and then starts the deal, her rings glittering as she expertly tosses the cards on the table. She knows the betting habits of most players so she's used to winning, sweeping away the piles of gold on the table to add to her riches. Before she starts the play, she rubs the gold ring on her right hand given to her by a Yankee trader for good luck. And so, the game begins.

Barcélo Palace is a gambling palace but it is also a place to enjoy popular regional fare, including *picadillo* (a mixture of minced meat, raisins, chile and spices that dates to medieval Spanish cookery), and *sopapillas* (soft pillows of fried dough dipped into a cinnamon-spiced caramel syrup). There are also *albóndigas* (Spanish meatballs), *carne adovada* (pickled meat), *arroz con pollo* (rice with chicken) and tamales, both savory—stuffed with chicken or pork and topped with a red chile sauce—and sweet, with mincemeat, piñon nuts and raisins. Tamales have drifted up from Mexico, where they were a staple in Montezuma's Court, made with maize flowers, ground amaranth seed and cherries or stuffed with roast turkey, hen or quail.

Though she loves all the rich foods of New Mexico, Doña Tules is of thin stature, hence her nickname *La Tules* (the reed). She loves to shop the outdoor markets in Santa Fe for green and red chile, corn, onions, beans, cheese, eggs, and seasonal orchard fruit including peaches, apples, apricots and plums from local farmers. She uses fruit that dries and stores well throughout the winter as fillings in pastry.

Like other wealthy residents, La Tules enjoys a late afternoon snack much like British high tea. But in Santa Fe, the four o'clock drink of choice is hot chocolate, traditionally served with *molettes,*—sweet rolls made with sugar, eggs, lard and a sprinkling of anise or saffron. The beverage is so popular that some residents have added chocolate rooms to their houses where the delicacy is ground, and then served as a beverage mixed with honey, cinnamon and cloves.

There's no doubt that she's become powerful over the years. Because of her affair with Manuel Armijo, the last Mexican governor of New Mexico, La Tules

THE SPANISH PALATE

The Spanish introduced the region to domesticated cattle, goats, sheep, pigs, geese and chickens as well as wheat and herbs, including wild marjoram, oregano and yerba buena (wild mint) prized both for their flavors and healing powers. They established orchards in northern New Mexico and grew apricots, pears, apples, plums, quince and cherries. Villagers raised sheep and goats and made cheese from fresh milk, including a moist curd cheese for enchiladas and quesadillas.

In the summer, families foraged for wild plums and berries and piñon nuts and grew zucchini, bell peppers, tomatoes, potatoes and melons. In the early fall, after a day of harvesting piñon nuts, they might have enjoyed a picnic of seasonal foods—homemade goat cheese, a roasted leg of kid served with fall's first red chile sauce and *buñuelos* (fried bread), eaten with home-pressed molasses and wild oregano.

was able to provide helpful intelligence to the U.S. during the Mexican-American War. She even loaned the U.S. Army money to pay its troops after invading New Mexico. As compensation for her help, she was given a military escort to the Victory Ball at La Fonda, attended by Santa Fe's elite. A small bit of payback for all the scorn she's received as a saloon-owner.

Another bit of payback will come much later, she knows, for she has secured a burial spot in the St. Francis Cathedral, assured by the newly-appointed Archbishop Jean Baptiste Lamy, the first archbishop of New Mexico. Her contributions to the church have assured that she will have a lavish funeral when that day comes, and Lamy has promised that she will be one of the last people buried beneath La Parroquia Church on the Plaza.

Yes, she chuckles softly, as she wins yet another round of monte, she has made an impression on Santa Fe and all who travel through it. She holds the cards in this town. No one can dispute that. She pulls her *rebozo* closer around her shoulders and reaches into a pouch tucked into her waist that holds a small bottle. From it, she pours a bit of powdered tobacco into an *hoja* (a piece of corn husk) and rolls herself a *cigaritta* to smoke.

Doña Tules scans the room as she smokes, aware that her table is the center of attention. Everyone comes to watch her play and amass her piles of gold. She's content with her fame and even her notoriety, and she knows that she's the reason for the saloon's success. She signals to one of her serving girls. It's time to order dinner and she requests one of her favorites—savory and sweet tamales—to sustain her through the next round of the game. It's going to be another long night. She picks up her deck of cards, shuffles and deals.

WARM FLOUR TORTILLAS

MAKES A DOZEN

Tortillas originated in Spain as a flat corn bread. After wheat was brought from Spain to the New World, flour tortillas became popular, too. The corn version is slightly thicker while the wheat version has a higher gluten content, making them less fragile. The recipe is so simple you may never use store-bought tortillas again.

2 cups flour
¼ teaspoon salt
1½ teaspoons baking powder
1 tablespoon lard
About ⅔ cup cold water
1-2 tablespoons butter

Preheat the oven to 200 degrees.

Mix the flour, salt and baking powder together in a medium bowl. Cut in the lard using a pastry cutter or fork, and then stir in the water to create a stiff dough.

Turn out the dough on a lightly floured board and knead until smooth, about 1 minute. Divide dough into 12 half-inch balls. Flatten and roll each ball into a 6-inch circle using a floured rolling pin or your hands.

Cook on a lightly greased griddle for about 1 minute on each side, until they have nice brown spots. Keep the cooked tortillas warm in the preheated oven until ready to serve. They can be stored in the refrigerator for up to several days.

PALACE PICADILLO

SERVES 4

This lovely dish, fragrant with cinnamon, raisins and almonds, is a perfect filling for empanaditas and tamales and also goes well with tortillas.

2 tablespoons olive oil
1 small onion, roughly chopped
2 cloves garlic, finely chopped
1 pound ground beef, or a mixture of ground beef and pork
1 cup canned tomatoes, diced
2 tablespoons vinegar
1 tablespoon brown sugar
1 teaspoon ground cinnamon
½ teaspoon ground cumin
¼ teaspoon ground cloves
½ teaspoon salt
½ teaspoon freshly ground black pepper
½ cup raisins
½ cup blanched, slivered almonds
Cilantro, for garnish (optional)

Heat the oil in a large pan over medium heat, add the onion and garlic and cook for about 5 minutes, stirring frequently until the onions turn translucent. Add the beef and cook until it begins to brown. Stir in the remaining ingredients, except for the raisins and almonds, and bring to a boil. Cover and simmer gently over medium heat for 30 minutes, stirring occasionally.

Remove the cover, stir in the raisins and almonds (reserving a tablespoon or 2 of each for garnish) and cook until the liquid is absorbed. Garnish with cilantro and serve.

TAMALES TULES

MAKES A DOZEN

Tamales have long been a staple of New Mexico cuisine, traditionally served during the holidays and for special occasions. This recipe offers a sweet version, but you can also fill them with savory stuffings, including the Palace Picadillo.

20 cornhusks

1¾ cups masa harina

1 cup plus 2 tablespoons hot water (for mixing with the masa harina)

2 cups fresh corn kernels (or one 15-ounce can of creamed corn
    or 16 ounces frozen corn)

½ cup (1 stick) salted butter, cut into small pieces

2 tablespoons sugar

1½ teaspoons baking powder

¼ teaspoon salt

2 poblano chile peppers, roasted, peeled and chopped (see Kitchen Clue)

½ cup Monterey Jack cheese, shredded

¼ cup raisins

¼ cup piñon nuts, lightly toasted in small pan

Fill a large saucepan three-quarters full with water and bring to a boil. Remove the saucepan from the heat and place the cornhusks in the water, using weights to hold them down so they're completely submerged. Let soak for ½ hour, then drain.

Mix the masa harina and the hot water in a large bowl and let cool. Transfer to a food processor, and pulse a few times, until it forms a coarse puree. Add the corn, butter, sugar, baking powder and salt, and pulse a few times, and then let run for a minute or two until mixture is well-blended and fluffy. Stir in the chopped chile.

Line a steamer with cornhusks. Place the steamer inside a larger pan, and add water to the pan so it comes to just below the steamer.

Tear two of the husks into long thin strips for tying the tamales.

On a work surface, use one cornhusk at a time to assemble your tamales.

Place approximately 3 tablespoons of the masa harina mixture on top of the cornhusk and form into a long rectangular shape, leaving a 1/2-inch border on the tapering end of the husk and a 3/4-inch border along the sides. Sprinkle with shredded cheese, raisins and piñon nuts. Fold in the sides, then fold up the bottom end. Loosely tie a strip of husk around the top of the tamale, and place upright in the steamer.

When all of the tamales are wrapped and ready, cover the pan and steam until the filling easily pulls away from the husks, 1 to 1 1/2 hours. Be sure to check the pan frequently to ensure the water doesn't boil away.

KITCHEN CLUE

Make your own **roasted chile** with nothing but some heat and a paper bag. This makes them easy to peel. First, preheat the oven to broil. Place the whole chiles on a baking sheet lined with aluminum foil and broil, about 8 minutes per side, until skin is black and blistering. Place the chiles in a small paper bag, close tightly and let sit for about 20 minutes. Wearing rubber gloves, remove the chiles from the bag, and carefully remove the seeds and peel them, being sure not to rub your eyes! Now, they should be easy to slice and dice. You can store these in plastic bags in the freezer for up to several months.

THE IMMORTAL DOÑA TULES

The legendary La Tules died on January 17, 1852, at age 47. Her story has inspired many re-tellings, including *The Golden Quicksand*, a 1936 novel by Anna Burr, who portrays her as conniving and manipulative; Ruth Laughlin's 1948 novel, *The Wind Leaves No Shadow*; and *Viva Santa Fe!*, a play about her that was performed at the 1992 World's Fair in Spain. Santa Fe's gambling queen is also the namesake of a New Mexico wine, La Doña Tules Sweet Red Wine, made by Las Nueve Niñas Winery in the Mora Valley. The building that once housed her gambling palace still stands today at 142 West Palace Avenue in Santa Fe.

LA DOÑA'S MEXICAN HOT CHOCOLATE

SERVES 2

This traditional recipe is spiced with cinnamon, cloves, coffee and honey and makes a comforting, fragrant drink. You can substitute other kinds of chocolate, but the Ibarra has a unique flavor.

2 cups milk
1 cup heavy cream
4 tablespoons sugar
2 wedges Mexican-style chocolate, grated
1 teaspoon vanilla extract
1 teaspoon ground cinnamon
Pinch of ground nutmeg
Pinch of ground allspice
Pinch of salt
1 egg
4 cinnamon sticks, for garnish

Place the milk, heavy cream and sugar in a medium saucepan and bring to a simmer over medium heat. Remove from the heat and stir in the chocolate until melted. Stir in the vanilla, cinnamon, nutmeg, allspice and salt.

In a separate bowl, beat the egg with a handheld beater for a minute or so, until frothy. Pour the egg mixture over the chocolate and beat until foamy. Serve in mugs with cinnamon sticks as stirrers.

CHAPTER THREE

SUSAN SHELBY MAGOFFIN, TEENAGE BRIDE ON THE SANTA FE TRAIL

(1846)

EIGHTEEN-YEAR-OLD SUSAN SHELBY MAGOFFIN STROLLS ACROSS THE PLAZA WEARING her best bonnet and shawl, on the arm of her husband, 45-year-old American trader and agent, Samuel Magoffin. He and his brother, James Magoffin, are two of the most prominent traders on the Santa Fe Trail. The brothers have traveled as far south as Mexico City, establishing stores in Chihuahua and Saltillo. Susan's long black hair is pulled back in a simple bun and she's wearing an elegant brocade dress. After more than a month traveling the trail by wagon, she and her husband are staying briefly in Santa Fe, and have been invited to an elegant Mexican dinner at the home of General and Mrs. Leitensdorfer.

Three *señoras* greet them at the front door and lead them to the dining room, where a group is seated on cushioned benches, enjoying dainty *viands*. As is customary, the ladies are seated in a group on one side, and the gentlemen on the other.

The first course is soon served, *sopa de arroz*, a traditional early New Mexican dish of boiled rice dressed with slices of boiled eggs, followed by *sopa de otra* (other kind of soup). It's traditional here to eat something light before dining on heavier fare. The weightier dishes include *carne adovada* (pork cooked in red chile sauce), and *carne de cocida* (roasted, boiled meat) along with endless glasses of champagne. For dessert, they enjoy rice pudding made with boiled milk, cinnamon and nutmeg.

After the final course, the general toasts, "To the U.S. And Mexico! We are now united, may no one ever think of separating!" and the guests rejoin with cries of "Viva! Viva!" It's a tense time as the U.S. has recently declared war on Mexico and, just a few days ago, General Stephen Kearney and the U.S. Army took Santa Fe without opposition and hoisted the American flag over the Plaza. Now, a tenuous truce is in place.

The dinner has lasted some three hours and Susan is ready to retire. After more than two months on the Santa Fe Trail they are now staying in a real house, a four-room Mexican house just off the Plaza in the shadow of the church. The house has whitewashed adobe walls and dirt floors. The main room has a plank ceiling and cushioned adobe benches along one wall. In the bedroom, two windows have shutters, perfect for closing out the bright sun for a midday siesta, a daily ritual that refreshes both the mind and the body and marks the passing of day to evening.

Susan savors many of the new foods she has tasted during this journey, which started when they left Independence, Missouri, and will end when they arrive in Mexico. She's tried tortillas, chile, chocolate, mutton, stewed chicken with cipollinis and a bread and grape dessert pudding. Then there was the oyster and champagne dinner! On the trail, Indian Pudding (atole with eggs, milk and molasses) is a staple, but Susan prefers capirotada, a Mexican bread pudding that descends from a favorite dish of the 17th-century prophet Mohammed.

She smiles, remembering her first taste of green chile stew. It had sickened both her heart and her stomach, and a few bites were all she could take. But the strength of it. The foreign-ness of it. This had stayed with her and eventually won her over. She had the same reaction to New Mexico cheese—very tough and unpalatable. But now she's so taken with the regional cuisine that she's thinking of writing a cookery book so her friends in the States can savor the cuisine she's discovered in this strange, new land.

The dusty town's outdoor markets have enchanted her, full of summer's harvest—huge quantities of chile, *sandias* (watermelons), *huevos* (eggs), *queso* (cheese), piñon nuts and fresh bread. There are also fine grapes from local vineyards, brought to market in wicker baskets on the backs of burros. And she's spotted bacon, ham, oysters, mackerel, cheese, raisins, coffee, sugar, molasses and champagne. So much delightful food.

Oh, she has lots to write about in the diary she's been keeping, chronicling their trip. Riding in a bumpy wagon, sleeping in a tent with their greyhound, Ring, keeping vigil. Eating simple breakfasts of bread and coffee prepared on a campfire. The wagons carrying so much food—barrels of flour, 150 pounds salt pork, 100 pounds dried corn, 25 pounds of green apples, a barrel of molasses, a keg of beef suet to use as butter and a chicken coop! Wealthier travelers indulging in oysters, sardines, wine from the Canary Islands and French champagne... And oh, the people she's met in Santa Fe. That infamous Doña Tules and her Barcélo Palace...

Wasn't it a grand decision to join her husband on this journey? Susan never imagined that marrying Samuel, the son of a prosperous Irish immigrant, would have led her to this. To visit these mesas of the Southwest that she had read about as a child? And, the fresh prairie air? It is all so good for her. Such an adventure!

What a far cry from where she grew up, on a plantation outside of Danville, Kentucky. Her grandfather, Isaac Shelby, was an American Revolutionary War hero and the first governor of Kentucky.

Soon Susan and Samuel will be traveling down the Santa Fe Trail once again, headed into Mexico, where there is great demand for the goods they bring—clothing, books, a printing press and other staples. But for now she's going to enjoy the respite--the shopping, the cooking, the entertaining, the writing in her journal. Along with fur and silver, the diary will be one of the things that endures the long journey.

SUSAN MAGOFFIN'S DIARY

After leaving Santa Fe on Oct. 7, 1846, the Magoffins headed south to El Paso del Norte, Chihuahua and Saltillo. The journey took its toll on Susan's health. She grew sick with yellow fever in Chihuahua and had a son who did not survive. The couple returned to Kentucky in 1848, then moved to a large estate near Kirkwood, Missouri. Susan gave birth to two daughters, and died on October 26, 1855, shortly after the second one was born. She is buried in Bellefontaine Cemetery in St. Louis.

Susan kept a journal of her journey along the Santa Fe Trail, as she and her husband traveled in the wake of the invading U.S. Army heading to Mexico during the Mexican-American War of 1846-1848. *Down the Santa Fe Trail and Into Mexico: The Diary of Susan Shelby Magoffin, 1846-1847* is a valuable source of information about life on the trail, as well as people and events of the time, and it also provides a rare woman's perspective of this fascinating era.

While Susan wasn't writing for publication, she seemed to know that her journal would be read. But it wasn't published until 1926, when librarian Stella M. Drum of the Missouri Historical Society, persuaded Susan's daughter to allow its printing. Today, the diary is a classic work used by scholars and historians studying the period.

SANTA FE TRAIL FRIED GRITS

SERVES 4

Grits, a staple along the Santa Fe Trail, were served in a variety of ways—topped with butter and maple syrup or molasses, or as a savory dish with gravy or tomato jam.

5 cups water
½ teaspoon salt
1 cup stone ground grits
½ cup all-purpose flour
Olive oil for frying

Bring the water and salt to a boil in a large saucepan and stir in the grits. Reduce the heat to a simmer and cook, stirring constantly for about 15 minutes, or until the grits are thick and mushy. Add more water, if needed.

Butter a 9x13-inch baking dish, and pour in the grits. Cover and cool to room temperature, then refrigerate until thoroughly chilled and firm, about 1 hour.

Spread flour into a shallow pan. Cut the grits into rectangles, and then dredge through the flour, shaking off any excess.

Add the olive oil to a large pan to a depth of 1/2-inch and heat over medium-high. Fry each piece for about 2 minutes per side, until honey brown. Drain on paper towels, sprinkle with salt, and serve hot.

TOMATO JAM

MAKES ABOUT 2 CUPS

This aromatic jam, flavored with spices and brown sugar, is delicious spread on tortillas, served with scrambled eggs and goat cheese, or with steak or pork.

6 large ripe tomatoes, peeled and roughly chopped, with juice
½ cup Muscavado sugar, or to taste (See Kitchen Clue)
4 tablespoons lime juice, freshly squeezed
1 teaspoon fresh ginger, finely grated
½ teaspoon ground cinnamon
½ teaspoon ground cloves
½ teaspoon salt
Pinch of red pepper flakes

Combine all of the ingredients in a non-reactive saucepan and bring to a boil. Reduce the heat and simmer, stirring often, until the jam reduces and thickens, about 1 hour. Remove from the heat and cool.

KITCHEN CLUE

Muscovado sugar, also known as Barbados sugar, is the darkest variety of brown sugar. It hails from Barbados but became popular in England, and is created by drying sugar crystals in the sun or under a low heat source. This process allows the sugar to retain more plant material, creating a stickiness and a heavy molasses flavor. Muscovado is often used in gingerbread and other ginger recipes. Here, it provides a richer flavor than regular brown or white sugar that complements the spices and tomatoes.

CARNE ADOVADA

SERVES 4

This traditional Mexican dish remains popular in New Mexico—rich and hearty, served with tortillas, posole, or rice and beans. If you can marinate it for 48 hours, it's worth the wait.

2 tablespoons olive oil
2 garlic cloves, minced
2 tablespoons flour
½ cup chile powder
2 cups beef broth
½ teaspoon salt
¼ teaspoon freshly ground black pepper
2 tablespoons sherry vinegar or red wine vinegar
1 tablespoon honey
1 pound pork roast, cubed

Heat the oil in a large pot over medium heat and cook the garlic until fragrant, about 1 minute. Stir in the flour, then the chile powder, and mix well. Add the broth then simmer until slightly thickened. Add the vinegar, honey, salt and pepper. Combine the pork with the red chile sauce in a large bowl, cover with plastic wrap and marinate for 24 hours.

Preheat oven to 350 degrees. Place the pork and the marinade in an oven-proof dish and bake uncovered for about 2 hours.

CAPIROTADA

SERVES 6-8

This Mexican version of bread pudding is layered with cheese and soaked in a brown sugar sauce. It was popular with travelers on the portion of the Santa Fe Trail that led into Mexico.

8 ounces good French bread—one small loaf or 6 French rolls
1 cup light brown sugar
1½ cups water
1 teaspoon ground cinnamon
4 tablespoons sweet butter
1 cup sweet wine, preferably Madeira
¾ cup dark raisins
¾ cup piñon nuts
1 cup shredded Monterey Jack cheese
Cinnamon-Scented Whipped Cream (see page 38)

Preheat oven to 350 degrees. Butter a 9x13-inch baking dish.

Tear the bread into bite-size pieces, place on a baking sheet in a single layer and toast lightly in oven for about 10 minutes, stirring occasionally.

Cook the brown sugar in a heavy saucepan over medium heat without stirring, until it begins to dissolve then start to stir using a metal spoon. Turn the heat to low as the sugar melts and stir until it's completely dissolved and the color of dark honey. Be sure not to let it burn.

Remove the pan from the heat and stir in the water, 1 teaspoonful at a time, until the mixture turns syrupy. If there are lumps, put the pan back on the heat and boil until they dissolve. Stir in the cinnamon and butter while the sauce is still hot.

Put the toasted bread in a baking pan and spoon the wine over each piece. Sprinkle the raisins, piñon nuts and cheese on top. Pour the caramel syrup over the top and bake for 30 minutes. Serve with Cinnamon-Scented Whipped Cream.

CINNAMON-SCENTED WHIPPED CREAM

MAKES 2 CUPS

This frothy version of whipped cream is enhanced with cinnamon and vanilla, and it's a perfect side note to cakes, pies and other desserts. It's also delicious in coffee drinks.

1 cup heavy cream
2 tablespoons confectioners' sugar
1 teaspoon ground cinnamon
¼ teaspoon vanilla extract

Whip the cream in a medium bowl using an electric mixer, or a hand-held beater, until medium soft peaks form. Gently stir in the sugar, cinnamon and vanilla. Keep chilled until you're ready to use.

OYSTERS ON
THE SANTA FE TRAIL

Oysters were popular along the Santa Fe Trail, and they traveled in two ways—in tin cans during the trail's early years and later, fresh, packed in barrels with their shells pointing up so they could be fed cornmeal, sprinkled on top of ice, which carried it to the oysters' mouths as it melted. The resulting oysters were fatter when they got to Santa Fe than when they left the Chesapeake Bay.

CHAPTER FOUR

BILLY THE KID,
WILD WEST GUNFIGHTER
(1879)

"There's many a slip 'twixt the cup and the lip."

BILLY THE KID

BILLY THE KID LOOKS OUT THE WINDOW OF HIS HOTEL ROOM IN LAS VEGAS, NEW Mexico, watching for any officers of the law on the busy street below. He's holed up here, an outlaw, after yet another escape from jail. He had come out of hiding after Lew Wallace, the new governor of the New Mexico Territory, had promised Billy amnesty in exchange for his testimony about the Lincoln County War, the bloody battle in southern New Mexico between two rival merchant factions.

Billy had met with Wallace in Lincoln County to discuss a possible amnesty deal. He showed up—his Winchester '73 rifle in one hand and his favorite compact .41-caliber Colt double-action Thunderer revolver in the other—and listened to the governor explain that he would grant immunity if Billy agreed to a token arrest, a short stay in jail until he concluded his testimony.

But instead of being set free after his testimony, he was ordered jailed by district attorney William Rynerson, an ally of Billy's enemy in the Lincoln County War. And what else could he do but escape, yet again? Now he's hiding in Las Vegas, playing monte at the new gambling halls and hotels. His friend, Jesse James, is in town and the two have plans to meet for dinner at the nearby hot springs resort.

THE LEGEND OF BILLY THE KID

Billy the Kid met his match at midnight on July 14, 1881, in Fort Sumner, when hunger drove him from the kitchen and into his friend Pete Maxwell's house in search of a newly slaughtered yearling to cook for dinner. Barefoot and bare-headed, he stepped onto the porch where two of Sheriff Pat Garrett's men were seated as lookouts. Unaware, Billy continued into the house and then into Pete's bedroom, where the sheriff sat quietly waiting for him. "*Quién es?*" "Who's there?" Billy asked several times. "It's him," Maxwell is said to have whispered to Garrett, who then shot the Kid.

At least, that's the official version of the story. But legends persist that Billy the Kid was never shot by Garrett and that he escaped to live out his life elsewhere, anonymously, possibly in upstate New York.

Billy was only 21 and already a legend of the Wild West at the time of his reported death. Members of Hispano communities, many of whom had sheltered him from the law, greatly mourned his death and compared him to Robin Hood, a fighter for the downtrodden. He's inspired more movies than any other figure in popular culture, including *Young Guns* and numerous documentaries. The short story, *The Caballeros Way*, by O. Henry is based on him, as is Aaron Copeland's ballet, *Billy the Kid*.

Billy is used to a hardscrabble life. When he was 15, he got caught stealing a few pounds of butter from a rancher in Silver City. Another theft got him thrown in jail, where he pulled off his first escape by climbing out through a chimney.

He's lithe as a cat, and he stays sharp by avoiding liquor. Heck, he doesn't even smoke. But he does have a weakness for the Spanish card game, monte, and he's good at it, too. He's also a crack shot and has no problem bagging turkey, deer and even a bear or two. He loves New Mexican food, especially tamales and warm tortillas, frijoles and posole. He carries a few of his favorite desserts, fruit turnovers, in his saddlebag for whenever his sweet tooth strikes.

Billy also loves to sing and dance waltzes, polkas and squares. His favorite song is "Turkey in the Straw"—and he has a lilting tenor voice that's as pretty as a bird's, he's been told. With his ice-blue eyes, curly, sandy brown hair, and skin tanned the color of chestnut, he draws the eyes of lots of pretty gals. He's fluent in Spanish, which makes him popular with the *señoritas*. His love of pretty women has sometimes gotten him into trouble.

But then his whole life has been nothing but trouble, starting in the Irish slums of New York City, where he was born Henry McCarty. His mother, Catherine, moved the family to Indianapolis, where she met William Antrim. They moved together to Wichita in 1870. There they fished for carp and catfish and also ate venison, prairie chickens, rabbits and buffalo hump, as this was the height of the U.S. Army's extermination of the buffalo on the plains and prairies.

In 1873 the family moved to the Territory of New Mexico, seeking a better climate for his mother, who suffered from tuberculosis. She and Antrim were married at the First Presbyterian Church in Santa Fe, then settled the family in Silver City, a mining boomtown. They lived in a cabin on Main Street, where noisy gamblers at the Red Onion, Blue Goose or the pricey Orleans Club kept Billy awake late at night.

A lot of his early days revolved around food. His stepfather worked as a butcher at Richard Knight's meat market and his mother sold the best fresh-baked pies, breads and sweet cakes in town. But when she died from tuberculosis in 1874, the family fell apart. Billy and his brother, Josie, were sent to foster homes, and Billy worked at a local hotel for a time, washing dishes and serving tables. Following his first jailbreak, he fled to the Arizona Territory in a perilous stagecoach journey. The food alone should have killed him—stale bread, greasy beef tougher than leather, even mule flesh!

It didn't take long for trouble to track him down. Confronted by a bully in a barroom brawl, Billy shot him dead and fled back to New Mexico, changing his name to William H. Bonney. He'd fallen in with the Jesse Evans gang, outlaws who taught him to steal horses and shoot like an expert. That's when he'd mastered the art of monte, and become known as "The Kid".

Billy moved to Lincoln, a one-street, one-horse town, where he found work in a cheese factory. Later, when he was caught stealing cattle, English cattle rancher and merchant, John Tunstall, hired him as a cattle guard. And that's how Billy got involved in the bloody Lincoln County War.

So now, after his failed attempt at amnesty from Governor Wallace and his subsequent escape, Billy's in Las Vegas, plotting his next move. He's spent a lot of time in Fort Sumner. It was there, on a recent visit, that he met a friendly barkeep from Texas named Pat Garrett, a buffalo hunter and trail driver. Fort Sumner is also where his friend, Pete Maxwell, has a ranch. Maybe he should go there next...

Billy has become a folk hero of sorts to the Spanish families of the region by fighting the Anglos who moved in and stole their land. And his popularity with the ladies is still strong. His friends joke that Billy has girlfriends all along the Pecos, but his favorite by far is Paulita Maxwell, Pete's sister. She's another reason to head back to Fort Sumner. He's heard she may be pregnant with his child.

Yes then, Fort Sumner it is. Billy grabs his signature Mexican sugarloaf sombrero with its wide green band and heads out into the night to play some cards and enjoy a proper steak dinner. He's had enough of the cowboy grub—son-of-a-gun-stew, biscuits and gravy. It's time to celebrate his freedom and look forward to the future.

THE LINCOLN COUNTY WAR (1878)

In Lincoln County, tension was thick between English cattle rancher and merchant John Tunstall and his business partner, Alexander McSween, and two tough Irish immigrants, Lawrence Murphy and James Dolan. With the help of the Santa Fe Ring—a corrupt group of politicians and business leaders—Murphy and Dolan ruled the county. The two ran a ring of thugs known as "The House," named after the mansion in Lincoln that served as their headquarters.

When Tunstall and McSween opened a general store on their turf, Murphy and Dolan sent a posse to kill Tunstall. Tunstall's men, including Billy the Kid, fought back, forming a group called "The Regulators," to avenge Tunstall's death. And thus began the Lincoln County War. Billy the Kid fought in almost every skirmish of the war until it ended in July 1878.

COWBOY BISCUITS

SERVES 4 TO 6

Biscuits and gravy helped many a cowboy and ranch hand get through grueling days in the Wild West. Dense and filling, served with beans and stew, biscuits were an essential part of any chuckwagon meal.

2 tablespoons each, flour and cornmeal, for baking sheet preparation
2 cups all-purpose flour
2 cups whole wheat pastry flour
4 teaspoons baking powder
1 teaspoon baking soda
1 teaspoon salt
12 tablespoons (1½ sticks) unsalted butter, chilled and cut into pieces
1½ cups cold buttermilk

Preheat oven to 425 degrees. Mix the flour and cornmeal together. Grease or line a baking sheet with parchment paper and sprinkle with the flour-cornmeal mixture.

Combine the flours, baking powder, baking soda and salt in a large mixing bowl. Cut the butter into the dry ingredients with a pastry cutter or fork until the mixture resembles coarse crumbs, with no large chunks of butter.

Add buttermilk and stir until just combined. Working quickly, turn dough out onto a lightly floured board and knead gently until it starts to hold together, about 1 minute. Using your hands, press dough into a rectangle, about 1-inch thick. Cut into squares and place on prepared baking sheet, about ½-inch apart. Bake for 15-18 minutes, until lightly browned. Serve warm.

SON-OF-A-GUN STEW

SERVES 4-6

A staple for cowboys, farmers and ranch hands, this hearty stew was most likely a dish that Billy the Kid ate when roaming the range, herding or stealing cattle. In this version, the stew is spiced with cinnamon, cloves, paprika and other fragrant herbs.

2 tablespoons flour
1 tablespoon paprika
2-3 tablespoons plus 1 teaspoon chile powder
2 teaspoons salt
1 teaspoon freshly ground black pepper
2½ pounds beef cubes
3 tablespoons butter
2 onions, sliced
1 garlic clove, minced
1 28-ounce can of tomatoes
1 tablespoon ground cinnamon
1 teaspoon ground cloves
1½ teaspoons dried, crushed red pepper flakes
2 cups potatoes, chopped
2 cups carrots, chopped

Mix the flour, paprika, 2-3 tablespoons chile powder, salt and pepper in a deep bowl. Dredge the beef cubes in this mixture.

Melt the butter in a Dutch oven over medium heat, and add the onion and garlic and cook until the onion is transparent, about 5 minutes. Add the tomatoes, remaining chile powder, cinnamon, cloves and crushed red pepper flakes. Reduce the heat to low, cover and simmer for 2 hours. Stir in the potatoes and carrots, and cook uncovered for about another hour.

THE KID'S FAVORITE FRUIT TURNOVERS

MAKES A DOZEN

The Kid used to tuck these treats into his saddlebags when out riding the hills of the Wild West, to satisfy his sweet tooth. He might have enjoyed them with a sweet apricot stuffing or the more savory mincemeat but you can use pie fillings too, including apple, peach and cherry. For a twist, mix a generous splash of brandy with the mincemeat or the apricot preserves before filling the turnovers.

Crust for one 9-inch pie:
8 tablespoons (1 stick) butter, chilled then cut into cubes
1¾ cup flour
¼ teaspoon salt
4-6 tablespoons ice water
Mincemeat (see recipe below) or 1 cup apricot preserves

Prepare the dough by combining the butter, flour and salt in a food processor and pulsing until the mixture is crumbly. Add the ice cold water in a slow and steady stream while pulsing until the mixture begins to pull away from the sides of the mixing bowl. (You may also do this step by hand, working the butter, flour and salt until crumbly, and then using a fork to combine the ice water.)

Turn the dough onto a lightly floured board and form into a ball. Cut into 4 quarters, and use the heel of your hand to smear each quarter, thoroughly mixing the butter into the dough. Roll the dough back into a ball and press into a 6-inch circle using your hands. Cover in plastic wrap and refrigerate 1 to 2 hours.

Preheat oven to 375 degrees. Line a baking sheet with parchment paper.

Remove dough from refrigerator. Turn the dough onto a lightly floured board and divide into two. Cut each part into 6 pieces (you will end up with 12 pieces of dough total), and use the heel of your hand to smash down each one. Roll each piece into a 6-inch diameter circle. Place 1-2 tablespoons of filling on one half of each circle of dough, then fold circle in half and use a fork to crimp edges together and to prick the top of each turnover. Bake on lined baking sheet for 20 minutes, until honey brown. Sprinkle with powdered sugar and serve warm or cold.

Mincemeat:
1 Granny Smith apple, peeled, cored and diced
⅓ cup golden raisins
⅓ cup dark raisins
⅓ cup dried currants
¼ cup dark brown sugar
¼ cup beef suet (or ¼ cup lard)
1 tablespoon lemon juice, freshly squeezed
1 teaspoon lemon zest
1 teaspoon orange zest
¼ teaspoon ground allspice
¼ teaspoon ground nutmeg

Combine all of the ingredients in a large mixing bowl. Chill in an airtight container for at least 3 days.

CAMPFIRE COFFEE

SERVES 4

The cowboys and outlaws of the Wild West made their coffee with a crushed egg, as the eggshells help the grounds to settle more quickly. It's just as easy to make over a campfire as it is to brew at home.

2 quarts cold water
1 cup ground coffee
1 egg
½ cup cold water

Bring 2 quarts cold water to a boil in a medium pot. Place the coffee grounds and uncracked egg in the middle of two overlapping 16-inch pieces of cheesecloth, and tie into a sack. Break the egg in the cheesecloth with a heavy spoon or your hand, and massage the bag so the eggshells blend with the coffee. Place the cheesecloth bag in the boiling water for 4 minutes. Remove from heat, and add ½ cup cold water to settle the grounds. Pour coffee through a fine sieve and serve.

CHAPTER FIVE

FRED HARVEY, CIVILIZER OF THE WEST

(1880s)

"3,000 Miles of Hospitality..."

FRED HARVEY'S MOTTO

NOT YET MIDNIGHT AND FRED HARVEY IS SEATED AT A TABLE IN THE GRAND DINING Room of the new Montezuma Hotel, just outside Las Vegas, New Mexico. Dapper with a Van Dyke beard and elegant Victorian gray suit, he's about to dig into the famous Harvey House midnight breakfast—a stack of plate-sized wheat cakes served with steak and eggs, hot apple pie and the best damn coffee in the country.

It's April 17, 1882, the opening night of Harvey's first luxury hotel. Built in the Queen Anne architectural style, it's named for the Aztec ruler who once lived among northern New Mexico's pueblos, according to local legend. Harvey has already delivered his keynote address, a toast to the largest resort he's built to date, with four stories, 270 guest rooms, a billiard hall, 11 bowling lanes, an eight-story tower, a miniature zoo and lawns for tennis, cricket, croquet and archery. A spa offers Russian and Turkish baths, mud packs and more, all fed by the magical healing waters piped in from the Montezuma Hot Springs. A brand new six-mile railroad spur from Las Vegas allows guests to travel by train all the way to the hotel's front entrance.

More than 400 people are in attendance on this opening night and the U.S. Army Band from nearby Fort Union plays for the ball, which likely will last

THE HARVEY GIRLS

If Fred Harvey thought his biggest challenge would be procuring fine, fresh food for places in the middle of nowhere or dealing with outlaws who held up the trains and depots, he was wrong. His hardest job was finding reliable help out in the Wild West. So he started advertising for waitresses back East and in the Midwest, looking for women ages 18 to 30, even though at the time, women worked mostly as maids or teachers. His wife met with each new hire to ensure she could live up to the strict etiquette standards, and thus the "Harvey Girl" was born.

Well-groomed, attractive, educated and impeccably trained in the "Harvey Way," these women served the meals in Harvey Houses across the country, wearing crisply starched black-and-white uniforms. They became so popular with diners that many of them married their customers, prompting Harvey to add a clause to his contract requiring a Harvey Girl to work at least six months before she could wed.

The Harvey Girl position became one of the most popular in the nation, with a salary of $17.50 per month along with free room, board and clean uniforms. It's estimated that some 100,000 Harvey Girls worked for the Fred Harvey company.

until early morning. The room glitters with eight crystal chandeliers as guests savor the remnants of the banquet—bluepoint oysters, spring lamb, beef tenderloin and truffles, salmon and trout, sweetbreads, venison with currant jelly and broiled tea duck—the finest food in the country prepared with ingredients purchased from farmers and suppliers who ship their goods twice a week in refrigerated cars. Some guests have already moved on to dessert—elaborate cheese plates, fruit pies, Queen of Puddings, Muscatine ice.

It's this kind of fine food, Harvey thinks, that is helping to make his vision a reality. A mission to build an empire that revolutionizes the way people travel across the country, one meal at a time. Before he launched his company, passengers had no other option for food but old meat, overcooked beans, soda biscuits so heavy they were known as "sinkers," and cold, week-old coffee, served in unkempt roadhouses. Now, thanks to him, travelers enjoy fine food prepared by chefs hand-plucked from the world's top restaurants and served by a staff selected from the best hotels in London, New York, Chicago and St. Louis.

Ingredients for his restaurants are brought in on the railroad and they're fresh and regional—oysters, prime beef and poultry, farm-fresh vegetables and fruits as well as exotic foods like green turtles and sea celery collected by pearl-divers of the Yaqui tribe. Presidents, princesses, dukes and dandies, entertainers and even foreign royalty are now regular patrons of Harvey's hotels, all arriving on the Atchison, Topeka & Santa Fe Railroad.

From such modest beginnings, Harvey has gone on to achieve high success. Born in Liverpool, England in 1835, he immigrated to New York at age 17 with only two pounds to his name. He landed a job at the popular restaurant, Smith & McNell's, where he worked his way up from dishwasher to line cook, receiving a solid education in the restaurant business. From New York he moved to New Orleans and then to St. Louis, where, in 1858, he took over the Merchants Dining Saloon and Restaurant and turned it into a bustling business. He was forced to close it down in 1861, when Missouri voted not to secede on the eve of the Civil War and chaos broke out in the city.

He then took a job as a railroad ticket and freight agent, and rode the rails tirelessly, experiencing first-hand the dismal conditions that travelers endured—sleeping in flea-bag hotels, eating grub served at railroad eating houses placed every 100 or so miles, when trains needed to stop for water and fuel. He knew that the staff at these roadhouses purposefully delayed the preparation of each order, leaving travelers no time to finish their meals so they could then recycle the same food for the next passengers.

Harvey believed he could do much better. He'd taken notes when he dined at the famous Logan House, a trackside hotel in Altoona, Pennsylvania, serving superb food. Then he'd made a deal with the AT&SF to run a second-story lunchroom in the railroad's depot in Topeka, Kansas, serving sandwiches, apple pie, other fresh fare and good coffee (a special blend created solely for his restaurants by Chase & Sanborn in Boston).

Harvey's standards are high. Ingredients must be fresh and portions generous. A 50-cent breakfast includes fruit or cereal, steak and eggs, hash browns and a stack of six pancakes with butter and maple syrup, followed by a slice of apple pie and coffee. His legendary ham sandwich, stacked with cheese and three slices of bread, sells for 15 cents. His secret? Don't slice the ham too thin! His 75-cent dinners feature wild game, beef tenderloin with mushrooms, Cornish game hens, roast chicken, Plantation Stew and hot biscuits, Sole Á la Normande and many other delicious dishes. His enterprise has done so well that the railroad has officially taken on the slogan, "Meals by Fred Harvey."

Harvey finishes his midnight breakfast and wipes his mouth with the edge of a signature Harvey House Irish linen napkin. He beckons the waitress for another round of wine and watches his guests continue their waltzing in front of the orchestra. Yes, this is a new jewel in his empire, this Montezuma Hotel. Now that it's open, he can turn to what's next in New Mexico. He's eyeing Albuquerque, Las Vegas, Lamy, Raton, Deming, Gallup and, of course, Santa Fe.

THE JEWELS OF THE HARVEY HOUSE EMPIRE

Fred Harvey died in 1901 from cancer at the age of 65, and his last words to his sons reportedly were "Don't cut the ham too thin, boys." The company continued on under the guidance of his sons and grandsons until 1968, when it was sold to the Hawaii-based hospitality conglomerate, Amfac, Inc.

At its peak, the Fred Harvey Company operated 84 Harvey Houses and 30 dining cars on the Santa Fe Railway. The restaurants became so popular that by the mid-1900s, they were using up a total of seven million pounds of potatoes, 1.5 million pounds of sugar, 500,000 pounds of butter, 750,000 chickens and 500,000 pounds of coffee per year.

La Castañeda, a Mission Revival-style Harvey House, opened in Las Vegas, New Mexico, in 1898, and was the site of Teddy Roosevelt's reunion of his Spanish-American War Rough Rider troops the following year. Other Harvey Houses in New Mexico included the Alvarado in Albuquerque (the first Harvey House designed by Mary Colter, famous for her interiors for the Grand Canyon's El Tovar and Bright Angel Lodge), La Fonda in Santa Fe, and El Ortiz in Lamy. With just eight guest rooms and a 112-seat dining room it was known as "the littlest hotel in the littlest town".

Starting in 1926, the shiny new Super Chief—the Southwestern-style flagship of the Atcheson, Topeka & Santa Fe (ATS&F) Railway—stopped daily at the Alvarado. Its 36-seat dining car served grilled and sautéed fish, steaks, lamb chops, caviar and champagne. By far the most popular dish was Pain Perdu, also known as Santa Fe French Toast.

FRED HARVEY FRENCH TOAST

SERVES 2

Santa Fe French Toast, the famous Harvey House breakfast dish, was created for the Santa Fe Railroad dining car in 1918. It was also known as Pain Perdu, a French term for "lost bread" since the dish traditionally is made with stale bread. This version is spiced with vanilla and cinnamon, and topped with fresh berries, applesauce and maple syrup.

2 eggs
½ cup light cream
½ teaspoon vanilla extract
½ teaspoon ground cinnamon
¼ teaspoon salt
4 thick slices of quality white or sourdough bread
2 tablespoons butter
2 tablespoons confectioners' sugar

Preheat oven to 350 degrees.

Combine the eggs, cream, vanilla, cinnamon and salt in a wide, shallow bowl. Soak the bread slices, one at a time, in mixture and set aside.

Heat the butter in a large pan over medium heat and add the bread slices, cooking about 3 minutes per side, or until golden brown.

Place the bread slices on a baking sheet and bake until the bread puffs up, 4-6 minutes. Sprinkle with confectioners' sugar and serve.

SPICED ORANGE PANCAKES

MAKES ABOUT A DOZEN PANCAKES

These light, deliciously spiced pancakes are inspired by the original recipe for the Harvey Girl Special Little Thin Orange Pancakes, invented at the Harvey House restaurant in the St. Louis station more than a century ago.

1 cup all-purpose flour
1½ tablespoons sugar
¾ teaspoons baking powder
¼ teaspoon salt
¼ teaspoon ground cinnamon
⅛ teaspoon ground cloves
1 egg, lightly beaten
¾ cup milk
1½ tablespoons butter, melted
1 teaspoon orange zest
¼ cup fresh orange, diced
6 tablespoons orange juice, freshly squeezed
Butter, for cooking
About ½ cup confectioners' sugar
Maple syrup, honey, sour cream

Preheat oven to 200 degrees.

Sift together the flour, sugar, baking powder and salt in a large mixing bowl. Stir in the cinnamon and cloves.

In a separate bowl mix together the egg, milk and melted butter. Combine the wet ingredients with the dry ingredients with a few swift strokes. Stir in the orange zest, diced orange and juice.

Melt about ½ tablespoon of butter in a large pan over medium heat. When the butter begins to bubble, add a heaping tablespoon of batter to the pan for each pancake. Be careful not to crowd the pan. Cook on the first side until bubbles appear, 3-4 minutes, then turn and cook for about 2 minutes more on the other side. Pancakes should be light brown and fragrant. Place cooked pancakes in the preheated oven to keep warm while you cook the full batch. Sprinkle with confectioners' sugar and serve with maple syrup, honey or sour cream.

ANGELS ON HORSEBACK

SERVES 4

A popular appetizer in the late 19th century, this dish is credited to a chef of German Emperor Wilhelm II. Early recipes suggest serving the dish on toast or on skewers. In this version, smoky paprika highlights the flavors of the oysters and bacon.

8 strips bacon
8 large oysters
Pinch of salt
½ cup flour
1 teaspoon smoked paprika
1 egg, beaten
½ cup bread crumbs
4 thin slices of white bread, cut on the diagonal and toasted
¼ cup fresh parsley, minced
1 lemon, cut into wedges

Cook the bacon in a large pan over medium heat until lightly brown on each side. Drain bacon using paper towels. Reserve a tablespoon or two of the bacon grease in the pan.

Dry the oysters with a paper towel and season with cayenne pepper and salt. Wrap each oyster in a strip of bacon and secure with toothpicks.

Combine the flour and paprika in a shallow bowl. In a separate shallow bowl, beat the egg with a fork or whisk. Place the bread crumbs in a third shallow bowl. Dip each bacon-wrapped oyster in the flour, then in the egg wash, and finally in the bread crumbs.

Reheat the pan with the bacon grease over medium heat and cook the oysters on both sides until brown, about 5 minutes total. Be careful not to burn the bacon. Serve on toast points garnished with parsley and lemon.

CHICKEN A LA CASTAÑEDA

SERVES 4

This recipe is a twist on a chicken dish from the famous La Castañeda Harvey House in Las Vegas, New Mexico. It's rich and hearty, topped with a classic Spanish sauce flavored with onions and garlic.

About 1¼ cup dried bread crumbs, plus more for topping
1 tablespoon butter
1 small onion, finely chopped
1 tablespoon flour
2 cups chicken broth
¼ cup cream
1 egg yolk
2 tablespoons fresh parsley, chopped
¼ teaspoon salt
¼ teaspoon freshly ground black pepper
2 large boneless, skinless chicken breasts
About ¼ cup olive oil
2 eggs, beaten
Tomato Frito (see recipe below)
¼ cup Parmesan cheese
¼ cup French peas, for garnish

Sprinkle a baking sheet with about ¼ cup of the bread crumbs.

Melt the butter in a pan over medium heat and cook the onions until translucent, about 5 minutes. Stir in the flour, and mix well. Add the chicken broth and cream, stirring constantly. Continuing to stir, bring sauce to a boil and cook until thick and creamy, about 10 minutes. Beat in the egg yolk, parsley, salt and pepper, and remove from heat.

Dip the chicken breasts into the sauce, coating both sides, and place on the baking pan sprinkled with bread crumbs. Cover the top of each chicken breast liberally with additional bread crumbs. Let cool completely.

Heat the olive oil in a large pan over medium high. As the oil heats, beat the eggs and place in a shallow dish. Dip each chicken breast into the beaten eggs, coating both sides.

Cook chicken breasts until golden brown on each side, about 10-15 minutes total. Serve with Tomato Frito, Parmesan cheese and French peas.

Tomato Frito:

This simple classic Spanish tomato sauce, with hints of garlic and onion, is incredibly versatile, complementing pasta, frittatas, poultry and meat. It's also great with grilled garlic bread.

3 tablespoons olive oil
1 medium yellow onion, diced
3-4 large ripe tomatoes, peeled and finely diced, with juice
1 teaspoon light brown sugar
½ teaspoon salt
½ teaspoon freshly ground black pepper

Heat the olive oil in a large pan over medium heat. Add the onions and cook until translucent, about 5 minutes. Stir in the tomatoes and juice, brown sugar, salt and pepper. Simmer uncovered until sauce thickens, about 45 minutes.

KITCHEN CLUE

Here's a simple, **sure-fire way to peel tomatoes.** Slit the bottoms with an "X" and drop each one, individually, in boiling water for 20 seconds. Remove and immediately place in cold water for another 20 seconds. Let cool and dry and *voila!*...each one peels easier than a banana.

CHAPTER SIX

MABEL DODGE LUHAN, TAOS ARTS MAVEN

(1920s)

"This is the provocative landscape that stirs the emotions...In this high valley, there is not a day that does not evoke the emotion of poesy, compounded as the surroundings are of beauty and terror, sun and shadow..."

MABEL DODGE LUHAN

LATE FALL IN TAOS AND MABEL DODGE LUHAN'S STOREROOM IS BRIMMING WITH THE bounty of the autumn harvest—apples to be made into pies, pudding, butter and jelly; pumpkins for soup; lamb and steer stored in ice chests for stews and roasts; oats and wheat from her fields; and jams, marmalades and preserves she's made herself from the fruits of her own gardens and orchards.

She surveys the options, considering what to serve her guests for dinner tonight. Author Willa Cather is staying in the Pink House, one of five guesthouses on her Taos estate, named Los Gallos after the Mexican ceramic chickens perched on the roof. (Her compound also includes stables, barns, corrals and a 1,200 square-foot gatehouse for the servants.) Writer Spud Johnson, publisher of the popular *Laughing Horse* magazine, lives just down the road and will join them, as will D.H. Lawrence and his wife, Freda, from nearby Lobo Ranch where they've been staying.

Mabel is a seasoned hostess among the world's movers and the shakers. She beguiles her guest with stories, wit and opinions, which she isn't afraid to share outright. Before coming to Taos in 1917, she presided over salons in her homes in both New York and Florence. Guests included writer Gertrude Stein, her partner Alice B. Toklas and her brother, Leo Stein; gallery owner and photographer Arthur Stieglitz; French novelist André Gide; activists Margaret Sanger and Emma Goldman and many others. But how different these salons were from her increasingly famous gatherings in Taos. At the villa in Florence, her dinner table included pitchers of wine and hot loaves of fresh-baked bread. In New York, each themed evening featured speakers and a lavish midnight buffet of cold meats and beverages. But life in Taos is not so cosmopolitan and her guests tend to stay for days instead of just a single evening.

Mabel discovered this remote outpost when she joined her third husband, Russian sculptor Maurice Sterne, who had traveled to Taos to visit the famous art colony and to sculpt. His urgent letter—that she must come immediately to see the Taos Pueblo Indians—brought her out on the train. She regarded the trip as a honeymoon of sorts, since they had been married only a few months when she banished him to Taos for admiring another woman.

But instead of celebrating a honeymoon with her husband, Mabel met Tony Lujan, the magnificent Taos Pueblo chief who changed everything for her the first time she visited Taos Pueblo. Wrapped in a wool blanket and seated by a fire, he was playing a water drum and singing, and she was utterly captivated. She would later claim that she fell in love with him right then and there, never mind that he had a wife, and she, a husband. And since that moment, her strange, new life has never ceased to startle her.

Taos is a mystical place for Mabel, along the lines of Atlantis or the Far East. She calls it her own Shangri-La. It's a fabled land where she's embraced a new way of life, a place that cracked her heart in half when she first saw it, a place more strange, terrible and sweet than any she had ever imagined. Mabel believes that Taos has connected her to an earlier way of life, one that belonged to her grandmother's generation, a life of extraordinary self-sufficiency. Even though it's hard work to plant, prune and harvest—and more expensive to fill up the storeroom and cellars with her own crops than to buy ingredients in the stores—Mabel believes it is critical to be in touch with her roots this way.

Through her connection to Tony Lujan (Mabel changed the "j" to an "h" when she married Tony, so it would be easier for her friends to pronounce it), Mabel is learning the Pueblo traditions honoring each season with ritual dances, drumming and singing. She firmly believes that the lifeways and traditions of Taos Pueblo can restore a Western world maddened by war and the mechanization of society. She sees the Pueblo people as "time-binders" who can reveal the true power of life. This is one of the reasons she has invited so many influential people to come and see the place for themselves.

Mabel brings the luminaries of the world to her Shangri-La, hoping they, too, will see that Pueblo culture holds an antidote to the problems that plague Western culture. Her guests include dancer Martha Graham, who was inspired to pioneer a new dance form by the dances she saw at Taos Pueblo and the Hispano folk dances in New Mexico. Psychiatrist Carl Jung also found fertile material at Taos Pueblo for his theory of archetypes, symbols of the collective unconscious. Ansel Adams was a pianist when he visited, and decided to become a photographer instead. And Georgia O'Keeffe painted her first works featuring New Mexico while staying at Mabel's.

Other visitors include poet Robinson Jeffers, playwright Thornton Wilder and novelist Vladimir Nabokov. And every guest is utterly entranced by the performances of dancers and drummers from Taos Pueblo at Mabel's house, by the readings, the music and the stimulating conversation.

Perhaps the most important guest she's lured to Taos has been British author D.H. Lawrence, whom Mabel calls Lorenzo. She wanted him to write a book about Taos Pueblo that would save Western civilization. She also wanted him to write a novel casting her as the heroine. But instead, he wrote the short story, "The Woman Who Rode Away," an unflattering portrait of Mabel as a woman kidnapped and killed by Indians, reflecting the animosity he felt towards her domineering ways.

Despite the tension between them, Mabel found the Lawrences a perfect place to stay high above Taos at Lobo Ranch, a rustic 19th-century homesteader's cabin with no electricity or running water. Mabel has no idea how he finds time to write up there. He tends a flock of chickens, milks his cows twice daily, bakes bread in an *horno*, an adobe oven, and follows the British habit of daily tea, brewing his own. For lunch, he makes salt meat, potatoes and applesauce and for dinner, porridge or cabbage soup and fried rabbit.

Dinner...Mabel realizes her guests will be here soon. She decides to serve a green chile lamb stew with savory biscuits and quince paste. For dessert, there will be fresh fruit and cheese. She wraps her shawl more tightly around her as the chill of the night settles in, and heads to the kitchen to make arrangements for the meal.

The kitchen is where her male guests typically eat their breakfast, seated at a big table covered by a blue oilcloth next to the wood stove. Most female guests, though, enjoy the luxury of breakfast in bed. Lunches and dinners are served in the dining room, where tall French windows let in natural light and the ceiling is painted with earth-colored stripes resembling a Pueblo Indian blanket. The black and sienna tilework on the floor was created by Santa Fe artist William Penhallow Henderson, the husband of Alice Corbin Henderson, who presides over the Santa Fe Writers' Colony. A heavy oak table with carved, studded leather chairs sits in the middle of the room.

The rest of Mabel's rambling adobe house is filled with furnishings from her 15th-century villa in Florence and her New York City brownstone—Venetian silks and Fortuny fabrics alongside Navajo rugs and Pueblo pots. Fragrant sweet peas, gladioli, geraniums and roses are scattered in vases throughout the house.

A banking heiress, born in Buffalo in 1869, Mabel grew up an unhappy, only child in the lap of luxury. She married early, left Buffalo, had a son, traveled to Europe and then moved to New York, where she became a central figure in intellectual circles. She's written anti-war articles and promoted the 1913 Armory Show in New York. She's survived a turbulent affair with journalist John Reed and three previous marriages. Now, she's living at the end of the world, a place where she's found more inspiration and happiness than anywhere else.

Yet change is in the air and Mabel can sense it. This stark, remote country has been discovered. Tourists are starting to overrun her beloved town, and even though some people now call Taos "Mabeltown," she's taken to calling it "Tinsel Land." This is partly her fault, as well as that of all her friends. Their desire to trumpet Taos to the world is beginning to create a backlash, and tourists now come seeking thrills instead of searching out the authentic life she first found so alluring. Is it too late to stop the transformation of her beloved home into a tourist trap?

It's definitely too late to be considering all this, she thinks. Time to get the dinner underway. Set the table. Light the candles. The sun has slipped beneath the horizon. The sky is becoming a canopy studded with infinite stars. Let the soirée begin!

SCHEMERS, SPIES
& A GERMAN COOK

When Mabel arrived in Taos during World War I, she rented rooms in an old, dark adobe house owned and occupied by eccentric British schemer Arthur Rochford Manby. He quickly became suspicious of her cook, who had a German last name, as well as her Russian husband and her frequent visits to Taos Pueblo. He assumed Mabel's trunks and boxes shipped from New York contained weapons.

Believing his tenants were part of a plot to persuade the Pueblo Indians to attack the U.S., Manby contacted a federal agent in Albuquerque who came to investigate. Mabel wrote about the incident in a letter to a friend: "We are in the maddest, most amusing country in the world—in the freakiest—most insane village your ever dreamed of & I would like to stay forever."

PUEBLO PUMPKIN SOUP

SERVES 6

This creamy, aromatic soup is perfect for an autumn night, flavored with shallots, onions, garlic and sage. You can substitute canned pumpkin for the roast pumpkin without sacrificing a lot of flavor.

1¾ pound sugar baby pumpkin, seeds removed and quartered or 2 cans pumpkin
1 tablespoon olive oil
¼ teaspoon salt
¼ teaspoon freshly ground black pepper
4 tablespoons butter
2 onions, finely diced
2 medium shallots, finely diced
2 cloves garlic, minced
6 cups vegetable stock
1 teaspoon ground dried sage
¼ cup heavy cream
Homemade croutons (see page 125)

Preheat oven to 350 degrees.

Rub the pumpkin flesh with olive oil, and season with salt and pepper. Place on a baking sheet and bake until soft, 30-40 minutes. Set aside to cool.

Melt the butter in a heavy stockpot over medium heat. Add the onions, shallots and garlic, and cook until onions start to turn translucent, about 5 minutes.

Using a spoon, scoop out pumpkin flesh, and stir into the onion mixture. Cook for 5 minutes. Add the vegetable stock and sage, and simmer uncovered for 30 minutes. Remove from heat, and stir in the cream. In a food processor (or using an immersion blender), purée until smooth. Serve with homemade croutons.

SAVORY PARMESAN BISCUITS

MAKES ABOUT A DOZEN

These biscuits are simple and delicious— flaky with a golden top, slathered in butter, quince paste or fruit preserves. They're also perfect for dunking in pumpkin soup.

1¾ cups all-purpose flour
2½ teaspoons baking powder
1 teaspoon coarse salt
6 tablespoons (¾ stick) chilled unsalted butter, cut into small pieces
¾ cup milk

Preheat oven to 450 degrees. Butter a baking sheet.

Stir together the flour, baking powder and salt in a medium bowl.

In a separate bowl, cut butter into flour using a fork until mixture resembles a coarse meal. Slowly add the milk, stirring until dough holds together.

For softer biscuits, drop dough into 2-tablespoon mounds onto baking sheet. For firmer biscuits, turn the dough out onto a clean, lightly floured surface and gently knead a few times. Roll out dough to about ¾-inch thick. Using a biscuit cutter or sturdy glass, cut out biscuits, re-rolling any scraps. Place on the buttered baking sheet and bake until honey brown, 13-15 minutes.

TAOS QUINCE PASTE

MAKES ABOUT 2 CUPS

This dish is eaten around the world. In Spain it's called "dulce de membrillo." In the Provence region of France, it's part of the annual Christmas feast, and in Israel, it's a traditional Sephardic dish.

3 cups quince (1.5 pounds)
2-3 cups sugar

Peel the quince, cut in half and remove the core and seeds. Slice into ¼-inch pieces, and place in a large pot. Cover with water and bring to a boil over high heat. Reduce the heat to low and cook, uncovered, for 30 to 40 minutes, or until the quince slices are tender and red. Let cool.

Put the quince slices through a food mill (don't use a food processor as it will make the texture too fine). Add the mixture to a medium saucepan and stir in the sugar. Cook over low heat, stirring, until the sugar dissolves. Continue to cook, uncovered, over low heat for about 1 hour, or until the mixture is thick and sticks to the spoon.

Preheat oven to 125 degrees. Grease a 9x13-inch baking dish.

Spread the quince mixture into the baking dish with a spatula and let cool. Place in oven and cook until it is dried out, about 1½ hours. Cool completely, and then slice and serve with manchego cheese.

LOS GALLOS GREEN CHILE LAMB STEW

SERVES 8

A rich and hearty stew, spiked with red wine and bearing the heat of green chile.

½ cup all-purpose flour
½ teaspoon salt
½ teaspoon freshly ground black pepper
3 pounds boneless leg of lamb, cut into 1½-inch cubes
4 tablespoons olive oil
2 onions, roughly chopped
4 cloves garlic, minced
½ cup red wine, such as Cabernet Sauvignon
2 pounds potatoes, peeled and chopped
6 cups chicken or beef broth
3 cups chopped roasted green chile
½ red bell pepper, diced

Put the flour in a wide, deep bowl and season with salt and pepper. Dredge the lamb in the seasoned flour and set aside.

Heat the oil in a large heavy pot over medium heat and, working in batches, cook the lamb until well-browned all over, about 8-10 minutes. Transfer meat to a separate bowl as it is browned. Using the same heavy pot, cook the onions and garlic for about 1 minute. Add the wine and stir to scrape the bottom of the pan to loosen any browned bits. Add the potatoes and broth. Return the meat and any accumulated juice to the pot. Bring to a boil, then reduce the heat and simmer until meat is tender enough to be pierced easily with a fork, about 1 hour. Stir in the green chile and red bell pepper and cook for another 20 minutes.

FIESTA FLAN

SERVES 6

Flan, which means "flat cake" in Latin, dates to the Roman Empire, when hens were raised solely for their eggs, and egg-based recipes were popular. The ancient Romans served the dish with a variety of ingredients. It was the Spanish who began the tradition of topping it with caramel.

¾ cup sugar
2-3 tablespoons water
4 large eggs
1 14-ounce can sweetened condensed milk
1 12-ounce can evaporated milk
2 tablespoons brewed coffee
¼ cup Mexican-style chocolate shavings
2 tablespoons cocoa powder

Preheat oven to 350 degrees.

Cook the sugar and water in a large saucepan over medium heat until it begins to melt. Lower the heat and cook until caramelized to a golden brown, swirling the pan so it melts evenly.

Pour carmelized sugar into a 9-inch cake pan, tilting the dish to evenly coat the bottom. Let cool and harden.

Place the cake pan in a larger roasting pan and add hot water so it comes halfway up the sides of the roasting pan.

Whisk the eggs in large bowl. Whisk in the condensed and evaporated milks. Pour into the cake pan and bake until it sets, about 50 minutes. Remove cake pan from roasting pan, and cool on a wire rack. Refrigerate until thoroughly chilled, at least 4 hours.

When ready to serve, run a knife around the rim of the flan to loosen it. Place a serving plate that's larger than the cake pan on top of the cake pan, then invert it over so the flan comes out onto the plate. Garnish with chocolate shavings and powdered cocoa.

CHAPTER SEVEN

GUSTAVE BAUMANN, HEART OF THE SANTA FE ART COLONY

(1930s)

"You could live a cocktail-party existence here; some do."

WINFIELD TOWNLEY SCOTT

A BEAUTIFUL MIDSUMMER NIGHT IN SANTA FE, AND ARTIST GUSTAVE BAUMANN AND his wife, Jane, are strolling the moonlit terrace beneath glowing paper lanterns at El Delirio, the White sisters' grand estate on Garcia Street. Sounds of laughter float on the air, mixed with the strains of Mexican music played by a trio on guitar, violin and mandolin.

El Delirio, named for a bar in Seville, is the hub of Santa Fe social life. Inspired by a mission church, it was designed and built during the 1920s by artist/architect William Penhallow Henderson (husband to poet Alice Corbin Henderson). An eclectic blend of Moorish, Mexican and Pueblo designs, it is the ideal setting for the sisters' varied celebrations—chamber music concerts, plays, masquerade balls, pool parties and lavish dinners.

Gus and Jane watch the party from the terrace with gin sours in hand. Amelia Elizabeth White, the elder sister, stands to one side, flanked by her beloved dogs, an Irish wolfhound and an Afghan hound, which the sisters breed and raise. Martha Root White is passing out finger food—smoked oyster puffs, oysters being a current Santa Fe fad; Spanish *albóndigitas* (tiny meatballs), all the rage; and empanaditas (fried pies stuffed with a variety of savory and sweet fillings), an eccentric menu perfect for one of Santa Fe's notorious bohemian parties.

But tonight, the Baumanns must leave early. They're due at one of artist Randall Davey's frequent dinner parties at his Upper Canyon Road home. Gus looks forward to swapping out the sweet drink he's been nursing at El Delirio for a glass of bootleg whiskey Davey keeps stocked in his bar. He's also anticipating a dinner of fish and game procured from one of Davey's hunting and fishing trips—maybe smoked trout and juniper-marinated, grilled venison along with fresh vegetables and fruits from his extensive gardens. The dinner party will be in full swing by now, Gus figures, Davey having completed his daily routine of painting followed by a two-hour horseback ride through the canyon and a late afternoon stop at La Fonda to play cello with friends.

Tomorrow night, Witter Bynner will host another of his infamously riotous parties, held on the Mexican-style patio of his rambling Buena Vista Street adobe home and in its rooms filled with Chinese carvings and Pueblo designs on the floors and ceilings. He often entertains his guests by playing a piano rolled up the street from La Fonda. Draped in turquoise and silver jewelry, he serves gin brewed in his bathtub, and is hardly recognizable as the scholar who wrote the definitive translation of Lao Tzu's work, *The Way of Life*. Before things get too wild, he'll politely ask his more modest guests to leave. Bynner's bashes are known to last for days and his many celebrated guests include Ansel Adams, Georgia O'Keeffe, Aldous Huxley, W.H. Auden and Edna St. Vincent Millay.

Still to come on the Baumann's social calendar is the annual party on August 4th hosted by artist John Sloan and his wife, Dolly. Following that there's the Poets' Round-Up Reading Series at Mary Austin's *Casa Querida* ("Beloved Home") on Camino del Monte Sol. Mary is one of the first American nature writers of the Southwest and a sort of mystic. "More like mystifying," Gus thinks, for though he's worked as a painter, set designer and director for the Santa Fe Community Theater, which she founded, he certainly finds her confounding. Take, for example, the vomitorium she had installed in her backyard, an invention from the Roman Empire era intended, she says, to aid in the discomforts of gluttony. People in her Santa Fe circle have taken to calling her "God's Mother-in-Law" because of her forceful personality.

The annual Fiesta celebration is just around the corner and Gus and his artist pal, Will Shuster, are building the giant puppet, Zozobra, whose dramatic demise by fire every years kicks off the annual festivities. Gus fashioned the first head of the giant marionette, whose name means "worry" in Spanish, and now the annual burning of Zozobra is as much a part of Fiesta as all the pomp, processions and parades.

Gus shakes his head in befuddlement. God knows how any serious artist or writer can get any work done in this town, he thinks. And he is serious about his art. A German-born woodcut artist and a leading figure in America's color woodcut revival, Gus was born in Magdeburg, Germany in 1881 and immigrated to America with his family at age 10. He grew up in Chicago, where he joined the Palette and Chisel Club and met Walter Ufer, Victor Higgins and Martin Jennings, now all prominent members of the Taos Society of Artists.

In 1918, Gus took the train to New Mexico to visit his artist friends in Taos. When he visited Santa Fe to see the new art museum, he fell in love with the town and ended up staying for good. He's achieved success with his art, and also with his whimsical troupe of hand-carved, painted marionettes, dressed in costumes sewn by his wife, who also writes the puppets' scripts. Gus created the puppets to entertain his young daughter, Ann, and her friends. They've become so popular that he and Jane tour the region, giving performances with characters and themes that reflect Santa Fe's cultural heritage. Their annual Christmas puppet show at the museum is a huge hit and in 1933, they performed at the Chicago World's Fair.

Gus would never live anywhere else, but an artist has to work to keep his focus! Friends get together almost daily for lunch or dinner at La Fonda, which offers three dining options—The Coronado Dining Room, La Cantina Cocktail Lounge and La Placita, an outdoor, Mexican-style terrace. The menu offers roast spring chicken with giblet gravy; a Mexican plate with tacos, tamales, enchiladas, salsa and a fried egg; French fried shrimp with tartar sauce; and pineapple fritters with brandy sauce. The

60-cent lunch special includes wine and mariachi music! Pulitzer Prize-winning author Oliver La Farge is there most days, in his broad-brimmed hat, discussing the latest political issues of the day. Nightly dancing in the New Mexican Room to the music of the Billy Palous Orchestra costs just 50 cents.

Gus and his friends also attend the annual masquerade balls at La Fonda hosted by the colony artists and writers. A recent Grand Jungle theme brought out more than 500 people, dressed in grass skirts, feathers and grease paint. Parrots danced with monkeys, missionaries with explorers, and Zulus with birds of paradise.

When they're not at La Fonda, the Santa Fe artists and writers frequent Canton Café and Burro Alley, a lively outdoor restaurant area, or George Pack's New Mexico Café at 125 San Francisco Street, known as "the place where artists and writers dine and talk."

Yet in other ways, Gus thinks, it's easy to be an artist in Santa Fe. Rooms rent for $10 a month, though hot water isn't guaranteed and the floors are likely uneven. You can buy a crumbling adobe for just a few hundred dollars and that's what many artists do, remodeling the houses themselves.

Most everyone keeps a horse in the front yard, butter in the well and piñon firewood for heat. The sound of a typewriter clattering away indicates a writer's residence. So many artists and writers live on Camino Monte Sol, the street has come to be known as "Artist's Row." This is where you'll find the famous *Los Cinco Pintores*, the "five nuts in adobe huts"—artists Fremont Ellis, Walter Mruk, Jozef Bakos, Willard Nash and Will Shuster. Around the corner, on Canyon Road, lives painter Olive Rush, who keeps a shed for her goats, as well as gardens, grape vines and cherry trees.

Baumann built his house in 1923. He sketched his own design, then hired architect T. Charles Gaastra, a fellow Chicagoan, to prepare the drawings. The house shows the influence of both Frank Lloyd Wright and the Arts & Crafts Movement in Baumann's hand-carved doorways, lintels and beams. His palette combines cream, ochre and green hues, along with turquoise and orange. In many of the rooms, he applied the paint himself, using a mottled technique with metal leaf and painted Pueblo imagery. He also built the shelves, cupboards, fire screens and gates.

The exterior, however, is unapologetically Southwestern in style; a one-story adobe with a screened porch where friends gather in the summer and a beautiful, octagonally-shaped gallery in the front for winter parties. The property includes extensive flower beds and an herb garden, where Jane grows her famous sweet woodruff to make May Wine. In the garden sits a concrete birdbath Gus sculpted in the shape of one of his Western hats. He loves the weeping mulberry, the Lombardy poplars, the Russian Olive trees roses, the lilacs, English ivy, Virginia Creeper and silver lace vines.

Yes, it's a good life in Santa Fe, Baumann thinks, gazing up at the inky star-studded sky, and he's grateful for it. He takes a sip of his gin sour and reaches for Jane's hand on the moonlit terrace at El Delirio. It's time to rejoin the party. And time to get ready for the next one...

A FROSTY BEER

In a legendary story still told in Santa Fe circles, Pulitzer Prize-winning poet Robert Frost visited Santa Fe in 1935 to present a literary lecture at the St. Francis Auditorium in the Museum of Fine Art, attended by some 200 people. Following the event, poet Witter Bynner invited Frost to lunch at his home, where the two got into an argument. Bynner, so incensed by the fame Frost had found—the fame that had eluded him—poured a glass of beer over the esteemed poet's head. Frost never visited Santa Fe again.

SANTA FE IN VOGUE

"You will find the more successful or the handsome-though-poor-ones at the smart tea-parties and the scornful young poets, the more determinedly 'modern' painters, and the 'proletarian' artists and writers renting a plumbingless mud house at ten dollars a month, with a yellow rosebush beside the well or plum-trees along the irrigation ditch, while the fashionable portrait-painter, the writer of best-sellers, or the blue-stocking may have the house next door, which has three bathrooms and a Spanish garden, and rents for two hundred dollars...Chummy, that's the word for Santa Fe social life!"

~Spud Johnson, *Vogue*, Oct. 15, 1936

ALBÓNDIGITAS, OR LITTLE SPANISH MEATBALLS

SERVES 4

These delicious meatballs are flavored with sage, mint, red chile and cilantro. They're great as an appetizer for 4 or a main course for 2, paired with a green salad or served with tortillas.

1 pound ground beef
½ pound ground pork
1 slice bread, soaked in water then squeezed out
1 egg
¼ teaspoon ground sage
¼ teaspoon dried ground mint
1 teaspoon chile powder, preferably Chimayó
½ teaspoon salt
½ teaspoon freshly ground black pepper
2 tablespoons olive oil
1 large onion, diced
1 garlic clove, minced
1 large fresh tomato, chopped
¼ teaspoon fresh cilantro, chopped
4 cups beef broth

Mix the ground beef and pork and bread together in a large mixing bowl. Stir in the egg, sage, mint, chile powder, salt and pepper and mix well. Shape into small balls, about the size of walnuts.

Heat the olive oil in a large pan over medium heat and cook the onions until lightly browned. Add the meatballs to the pan and cook until they turn golden brown and firm. Stir in the onion, garlic, tomato, cilantro and beef broth. Simmer, uncovered, 1½ hours.

GRILLED JUNIPER-MARINATED VENISON

SERVES 4

Pungent juniper berries, aromatic spices and red wine are a delicious complement to the gamey flavor of venison. This marinade works equally well with beef.

¾ cup red wine, such as Cabernet Sauvignon
¼ cup balsamic vinegar
3 tablespoons olive oil
2 tablespoons molasses
1 tablespoon crushed juniper berries (available in many grocery stores and online)
4 garlic cloves, minced
1 tablespoon orange zest
1 tablespoon lemon zest
2 bay leaves
2 tablespoons fresh thyme, minced
2 tablespoons fresh rosemary, minced
10 whole cloves
10 whole black peppercorns
¾ teaspoon salt
4 thick venison steaks (about 1½ inches thick)
4 fresh rosemary sprigs, for garnish

For the marinade, mix all of the ingredients except the steaks and rosemary sprigs in a medium bowl. Place the venison steaks and marinade in a large plastic bag, seal and refrigerate for 2 hours.

Strain the marinade through a fine sieve. Pour into a saucepan and bring to a boil. Set ½ cup of marinade aside for serving.

Place the steaks on a hot grill, basting frequently with the hot marinade, and cook for 6 to 7 minutes per side, until medium rare (145 degrees on a meat thermometer). Garnish with the rosemary sprigs and serve with the reserved marinade.

EL DELIRIO EMPANADITAS

MAKES ABOUT 3 DOZEN

Empanaditas are miniature empanadas, which originated in medieval Iberia during the Moorish invasions and were brought to the region of New Mexico by Spanish colonists. The name comes from the Spanish verb, emparer, which means "to wrap in bread." You can stuff them with a variety of foods, from meat and cheese to vegetables and fruits.

2 cups flour
1 teaspoon baking powder
½ teaspoon salt
½ cup lard
1/3 cup milk
Picadillo (see page 20), Carne Adovada (see page 33),
    Mincemeat (see page 50) or other filling
2 egg whites, lightly beaten

To make the dough, sift the flour, baking powder and salt together in a large bowl. Cut in the lard using a pastry cutter or a fork. Add the milk and stir until the dough pulls away from the bowl. Knead 2 or 3 times on a floured board. Using a floured rolling pin, roll out to about ¼-inch thick. Cut into 4-inch circles, using a round cookie cutter or a sturdy glass.

Preheat oven to 375 degrees. Lightly butter a baking sheet or line with parchment paper.

Place 1 tablespoon of the filling on half of each circle of dough. Fold over and crimp the edges with a fork.

In a small bowl, beat egg whites and brush on the top of each empanadita. Bake on the prepared baking sheet until golden brown, about 15 minutes.

THE WHITE SISTERS' LEGACY

Elizabeth and Martha White, the daughters of wealthy newspaper publisher Horace White, both attended Bryn Mawr College and served as army nurses in Europe during World War I. They first visited Santa Fe in 1923 and loved it so much, they bought property on Garcia Street and built their estate, which included a billiard house, guest houses, terraced gardens, a tennis court and a pool—Santa Fe's first. The sisters opened the first Native American art gallery in New York City and were crusaders for Pueblo Indian rights. Elizabeth had a prominent role in creating the Indian Arts Fund, the Santa Fe Indian Market, the Old Santa Fe Association, the Laboratory of Anthropology, the Wheelwright Museum, the Garcia Street Club, and the Santa Fe Animal Shelter. She was a proponent of Santa Fe Style architecture, Native American arts and crafts and Indian land rights and health care.

Martha died in 1937, but Elizabeth lived to the age of 96. Upon her death in 1972, she left El Delirio to the School for Advanced Research, on whose board she served for 25 years.

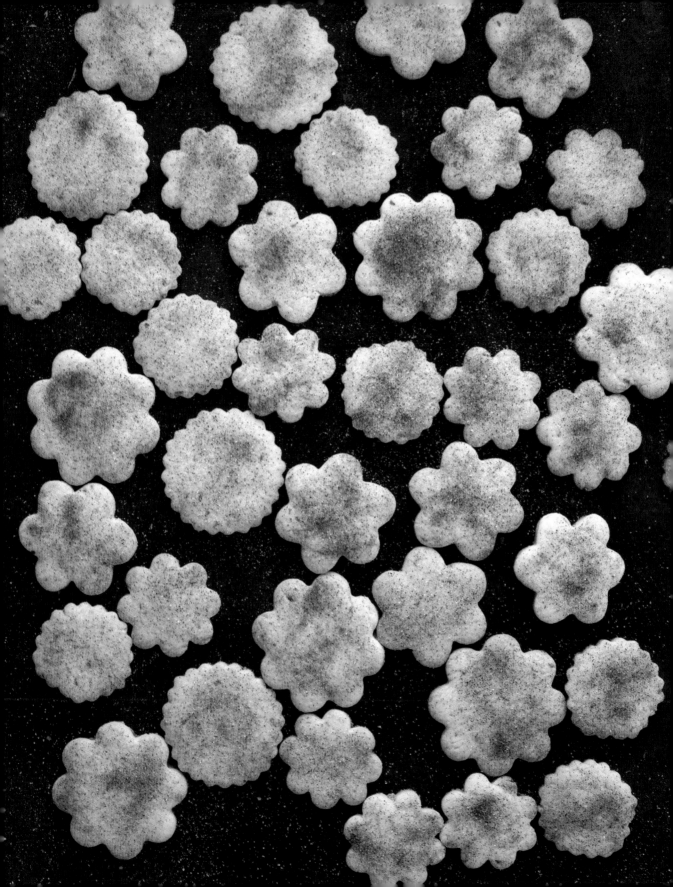

BAUMANN BIZCOCHITOS

MAKES ABOUT 6 DOZEN

This elegant cookie is a New Mexico holiday classic, and yes, you must use lard to get the perfect flakiness. Dusted with cinnamon sugar, and traditionally cut out in a fleur-de-lis shape, it is delicious.

1 cup lard, chilled
1 cup sugar
2 eggs
1 tablespoon anise seeds, crushed
1 teaspoon vanilla extract
4 cups all-purpose flour
2 teaspoons baking powder
½ teaspoon salt
¼ cup brandy, whiskey or sweet wine
1 teaspoon ground cinnamon
2 tablespoons sugar

Preheat oven to 375 degrees.

Butter a baking sheet or line it with parchment paper.

Cream the lard and sugar together using an electric beater in a large bowl until fluffy. Beat in the eggs, anise and vanilla.

In a separate bowl, sift together the flour, baking powder and salt. Stir the egg mixture into the flour mixture, add the liquor, and mix into a stiff dough.

Roll out the dough on a floured surface to about ¼-inch thick. Using a cookie cutter, cut out the cookies into desired shapes.

Combine the cinnamon and sugar in a bowl. Dunk the top of each cookie into the cinnamon-sugar mixture, and place on the prepared baking sheet. Bake until lightly browned, about 12 minutes. Cool on a wire rack.

CHAPTER EIGHT

EDITH WARNER, TEAHOUSE HOSTESS
(1940s)

"It was one of the strange aspects of Edith Warner's fate that brought these men and their wives from many nations to gather around her table."

PEGGY POND CHURCH

AS THE FIERY AUTUMN SUN SETS IN A BLAZE OF COLOR, EDITH WARNER LIGHTS the candles in the dining room of her teahouse at Otowi Crossing. Wearing glasses, thin of figure with narrow shoulders, her hair in limp coils, she sets the table with large terra-cotta plates from Mexico and black pottery serving bowls, in preparation for the arrival of Robert Oppenheimer, his wife Kitty, and whatever group of scientists working on the Manhattan Project he might bring with him.

In her brown buckskin moccasins, Edith darts from dining room to kitchen to stir an oversized pot of beef ragout simmering on the stove, its rich aroma filling the little house. A loaf of fresh-baked bread cools on the counter next to a big bowl of corn salad. In the oven, her famous chocolate loaf cake is nearly done.

A bowl of just-picked raspberries sits close by, to serve with the cake after dinner in hand-carved cottonwood bowls. She slices fresh lemon for spiced iced tea, then regards the line of jars along a shelf, deciding which will be best to serve tonight—her homemade sweet tomato jam, watermelon pickle, spiced peaches or other vegetables and fruits from her ample garden.

Tilano, her longtime companion from nearby San Ildefonso Pueblo, comes in the kitchen from outside, wearing jeans and a wrinkled cowboy hat, carrying wood for the fire. Edith asks him to set the coffee brewing, which he will serve after dinner as he shares jokes with the diners, his long black braids swinging.

Outside, a few cars drive up. It's the scientists getting out of their cars, a little rowdy, most likely from sharing a bottle of spirits on their drive down the winding dirt road from Los Alamos, as Edith doesn't serve alcohol.

She surveys the kitchen. Everything's ready. Even though she's been up since dawn preparing for tonight's meal—and she'll be up late into the night washing dishes with water heated on the stove in copper kettles—she's grateful to her visitors for providing her with such a wonderful war job. One beyond her wildest dreams. And she knows they appreciate her, too, for providing this respite from their high-pressured days and nights spent working on "the gadget," which is never, ever discussed during their visits.

When the U.S. Army had sought a remote site for its top-secret project—the project that had scientists working furiously to build the atomic bomb and end World War II—it chose the site of the Los Alamos Ranch School for Boys. Oppenheimer knew the area well, as his family owned a ranch near Pecos. The government bought the property, closed the school and opened Los Alamos on April 15, 1943. But most people living in Santa Fe and other nearby towns simply referred to it as "The Hill."

The scientists relish getting away from the tension of their jobs and savoring Edith's simple, hearty dinners and good conversation. Her cooking has become legendary, not just to the scientists but also to tourists on their way to Bandelier National Monument and to the boys who once attended the Los Alamos Ranch School.

Edith Warner was 30 years old when she left Pennsylvania in the fall of 1922, after suffering a nervous breakdown. Her doctor prescribed a year of outdoor life free of responsibilities and a friend who had visited Frijoles Lodge, west of Santa Fe suggested the place. As soon as Edith saw New Mexico, she decided she could live nowhere else. She found a job looking after freight at the tiny boxcar railroad station at the Otowi Switch, where the Chili Line (on its run between Santa Fe and Antonito, Colorado) stopped to deliver supplies to the Los Alamos Ranch School. She served as station mistress, postmistress and shopkeeper before the line closed in 1941. Now, her teahouse keeps her busier than ever.

In her house by the river, which she rents from famed San Ildefonso potter Maria Martinez and her husband, Edith makes her own jam and preserves from wild plum and chokecherry that she delivers in gaily-wrapped jars to the pueblo every Christmas Eve. She also cans fruit and vegetables and bakes her own bread and cookies. She often gives the surplus from her garden, along with her extra eggs, to the scientists' wives.

Her hearth is swept with a fireplace broom she made of hand-picked dried grass. Neat bundles of piñon wood provide kindling, which fills the house with its pungent fragrance. A Navajo rug covers part of the old, oft-scrubbed wood floors and the adobe fireplace displays glossy San Ildefonso black bowls on its graduated steps.

Edith has no electricity or indoor plumbing so she hauls water from a well using a rope and pulley. The well is also where she stores bottles of Coke, hanging them there to keep cool. She keeps her butter and milk in a "desert refrigerator," cooled by evaporation. Ice cream comes in on the train from Santa Fe.

Edith's one large dining table is booked months in advance, though Oppenheimer can always get a reservation. Dinner costs $2. If you can't get a reservation at Edith's place, options include the Mess Hall at Fuller Lodge for single diners, where the sprawling porch is popular. A café caters to married people and a cantina offers Cokes, beer, and light lunches.

These are tense times, indeed, so when the scientists need a break, they come to Edith's teahouse, and she's grateful for the company, the camaraderie and the friendship. She sets the table with oversized plates, brings out pitchers of spiced iced tea and fills a few pottery bowls with spiced apricots. The ragout, simmering on the stove, fills the room with fragrance, and her fresh bread is sliced and ready to serve. She can hear the laughter of her guests as they open the door and step inside, hungry and happy to be here.

LAST DAYS AT OTOWI

The world changed forever in a flash when the U.S. dropped atomic bombs on Hiroshima on August 6, 1945, and on Nagasaki on August 9. Los Alamos changed, too. Their job done, the scientists and their families returned home.

Once the news broke about the Manhattan Project, Edith Warner could confide to friends that Robert Oppenheimer, Neils Bohr, Enrico Fermi and so many others who worked on the bomb regularly dined at her teahouse. So many people from around the world—Germans, Hungarians, French, Swiss, Italians, Austrians and English.

After the Manhattan Project ended, Edith closed her teahouse and moved away from her home of more than 20 years to nearby Jacona. In her Christmas letter of 1950, shortly before her death from cancer, she wrote:

"How to endure the man-made devastating period in which we live and which seems almost as hopeless to control as drought; how to proceed ... but I know what depths of kindness and selflessness exist in my fellow man. Of this I have had renewed assurance recently, when those about me have shared self and substance. When Tilano lights the Christmas Eve fire, perhaps against a white hillside, I shall watch from the house where some have felt peace, and hope that in your sky there are some bright stars."

PAJARITO WATERMELON PICKLE

MAKES ABOUT 3 CUPS

Preserve the quintessential taste of summer with this delicious recipe, which blends watermelon with ginger, allspice and cloves as well as a dash of jalapeño heat.

1 4-pound watermelon
2 tablespoons plus 2 teaspoons salt
8 cups water
2 cups sugar
1 teaspoon fresh ginger, diced
1 jalapeño, diced
½ teaspoon pickling spice
¼ teaspoon ground allspice
2 cinnamon sticks
8 whole cloves
8 whole black peppercorns
1¼ cups apple cider vinegar

Cut the watermelon in half and scoop out the flesh and seeds. Scrape the rind with a metal spoon, leaving just a thin layer of pink flesh. Peel the green outer skin from the rind. Cut rind into 1-inch cubes. (You should have about 4 cups of rind.)

Bring 8 cups water and 2 tablespoons salt to boil in a large pot. Add the prepared rind and boil until tender, about 5 minutes. Strain and put the rinds into a large, non-reactive bowl.

Combine the remaining 2 teaspoons salt with sugar, ginger, jalapeño, pickling spice, allspice, cinnamon sticks, cloves, peppercorns and vinegar in a large saucepan. Bring to a boil, stirring until the sugar is dissolved. Pour the mixture over the rinds and place a heavy plate on top to keep them submerged. Cover and refrigerate overnight.

Strain the liquid and bring to a boil in a saucepan. Pour the hot liquid back over the rinds. Again, cover and refrigerate overnight. Repeat this process once more. Then chill in covered jars. The rinds will keep in the refrigerator for a few weeks.

A TALE OF TWO BOOKS

Atilano Montoya was governor of San Ildefonso Pueblo when he first visited Edith's house to build a fireplace in her tearoom. He was 60 years old, a widower and had traveled with a group of Indian dancers to display their dances in Europe—Paris, Rome, London, Berlin. The two had lots to talk about as they sat and became acquainted with each other. Soon, Tilano moved in with Edith, and though they never married and he was old enough to be her father, he was woven into her life as firmly as the land, the river, the mesa and the little house by the bridge.

Edith Warner's life in New Mexico inspired two acclaimed books: Peggy Pond Church's non-fiction *The House at Otowi Bridge* (1960) and the novel, *The Woman at Otowi Crossing*, by Frank Waters (1966). Both books present intriguing accounts of the life of this remarkable woman, but Waters' novel includes intimate, imagined scenes between Edith and Tilano, as well as of their fictional daughter. Waters's book angered the devotees of Peggy Pond Church's work who rejected his embellishments.

SPICED APRICOTS

MAKES ABOUT 2 CUPS

Apricots were brought to New Mexico by the Spanish and today grow abundantly in the region. There are many ways to prepare them, but this one is uniquely delicious, whether served with ice cream or pie or eaten alone.

2 tablespoons apple cider vinegar
1 whole star anise
1 cinnamon stick
1/8 teaspoon ground nutmeg
1/8 teaspoon ground cloves
2 cups dried apricots (or a 15-ounce of canned apricots), roughly chopped

Combine vinegar, star anise, cinnamon stick, nutmeg and cloves in a large saucepan and bring to a boil. Reduce heat, cover and simmer for 15 minutes. Remove from heat and stir in the apricots. Cover and let sit for 30 minutes, stirring often. Drain, if desired, and serve warm or cold. The apricots will keep for up to a week in jars, refrigerated.

OTOWI BRIDGE BEEF RAGOUT

SERVES 6

Edith Warner served a classic ragout much like this one to scientists from around the world who visited her simple teahouse for the camaraderie and conversation as well as reliably delicious food.

¼ cup all-purpose flour
½ teaspoon salt
½ teaspoon freshly ground black pepper
1 pound sirloin, cubed
4 tablespoons olive oil
1 large onion, thinly sliced
2 carrots, thinly sliced
1 celery stalk, thinly sliced
2 garlic cloves, minced
2 teaspoons dried oregano
2 bay leaves
2-3 large ripe tomatoes, peeled and diced, with juice (see Kitchen Clue, page 69)
1 cup red wine, preferably Cabernet Sauvignon

Combine the flour, salt and pepper in a wide-rimmed, shallow bowl. Dredge each piece of meat in the flour mixture and shake off any excess.

Heat 2 tablespoons of the olive oil in a large stockpot over medium heat and cook the meat for about 2 minutes, turning once. Remove from pan and set aside.

Add the remaining 2 tablespoons of oil to the pan and stir to combine with the drippings. Add the onion, carrots and celery and cook for 2 minutes, stirring frequently. Reduce the heat to simmer and cook for 10 minutes, stirring occasionally. Add the garlic and any leftover flour mixture and stir for 1 minute. Add the oregano, bay leaves, tomatoes and wine, and stir to combine. Then return meat to the pot. Bring to a simmer and cook until the vegetables are tender, about 45 minutes. Serve with a baguette or another variety of crusty bread.

SPICED ICED TEA

SERVES 8

A light, lovely beverage for a summer afternoon, spiced with cinnamon, cloves, orange and mint.

1 cinnamon stick
5 whole cloves
2 tablespoons dried orange peel
2 whole black peppercorns
6 black tea bags, strings removed
6 mint sprigs

Combine the cinnamon stick, cloves, orange peel and peppercorns in a small bowl. Place the spice mixture and teabags in a cheesecloth bag and tie with kitchen twine. Boil 8 cups of water, add the cheesecloth bag and steep for 5 minutes. Refrigerate until chilled and serve iced, garnished with mint sprigs.

TEAHOUSE CHOCOLATE CAKE

Inspired by Edith Warner's chocolate loaf cake recipe that is still being passed around, this recipe blends chocolate with coffee, almonds and cinnamon, topped with a decadent chocolate frosting.

¾ cup all-purpose flour

1¼ teaspoons baking powder

½ teaspoon salt

¼ cup ground almonds (see Kitchen Clue)

1 teaspoon ground cinnamon

½ cup (4 ounces) semi-sweet baking chocolate

2 tablespoons freshly brewed coffee

⅔ cup Vanilla Sugar (see Kitchen Clue, page 7)

½ cup whole milk

3 large eggs

1 teaspoon vanilla extract

Preheat oven to 200 degrees. Butter and flour a loaf pan.

Sift together the flour, baking powder, and salt in a medium bowl. Stir in the ground almonds and cinnamon.

Add the chocolate and coffee to the top part of a double boiler or small saucepan and cover. Place in a larger pan partially filled with water. Bring water to a boil. Remove from heat and let sit, covered, for about 10 minutes or until chocolate melts.

In a large bowl, beat the Vanilla Sugar and melted chocolate together using an electric beater on low until combined, about 1 minute. Gradually add the flour mixture and the milk, alternately a bit of each until well combined, and then beat for 1 minute. Add the eggs and vanilla, and beat for 1 minute more, until the batter has the texture of whipped cream.

Pour batter into the prepared loaf pan and bake for 15 minutes. Increase the oven temperature to 275 degrees and bake for an additional 15 minutes. Then increase the temperature to 300 degrees and bake for 30-40 minutes, or until a knife inserted in the center comes out clean.

Cool on a wire rack for 30 minutes, then remove the cake from the pan and cool completely. Cover with Chocolate Butter Frosting.

Chocolate Butter Frosting:
½ cup (4 ounces) semisweet baking chocolate
3 tablespoons freshly brewed coffee
8 tablespoons (1 stick) unsalted butter
½ teaspoon ground cinnamon

Add the chocolate, coffee and butter to the top part of a double boiler or a small saucepan and cover. Place in a larger pan partially filled with water. Bring water to a boil, then remove from heat and let sit, covered, for about 10 minutes or until all is melted and well-combined. Stir in cinnamon.

- For a thinner icing that can be poured over the cake, use as is.

- For a thicker, more spreadable icing place the pan with the icing into a larger bowl filled with ice water, making sure not to let any of the water spill into the icing. Beat until the mixture thickens. Spread onto the cake.

KITCHEN CLUE

Ground almonds are widely available, usually in bulk. To grind almonds yourself, measure the amount of blanched almonds you need and put in a food processor. For every ¼ cup of almonds, add 1 tablespoon sugar to keep the almonds from clumping up. You may use Vanilla Sugar for this if you like. Pulse a few times, until the mixture resembles coarse sand.

CHAPTER NINE

ROSALEA MURPHY, FOUNDER OF THE PINK ADOBE

(1950s)

"Creativity in the kitchen is a true art. Any basic recipe lends itself to subtle variations of flavor and texture that will bring pleasure to the guests—and fame and compliments to the cook."

ROSALEA MURPHY

IT'S FRIDAY NIGHT AT THE PINK ADOBE AND OWNER ROSALEA MURPHY SITS AT THE back table in the big dining room with a group of friends, taking a break from the kitchen. Her beloved dog, Richard, sits by her side while her two Siamese cats roam about, seeking attention. A black-haired beauty with striking green eyes and many admirers, Rosalea is dressed in her signature attire—a full skirt cut on the bias with a concho belt, a beautiful squash blossom necklace made of turquoise and silver, and oversized silver hoop earrings.

It's early fall, and tourists are still arriving in droves from Route 66, driving their shiny automobiles right up to her front door. They're eager to try the Pink's famous French onion soup and Steak Dunigan, a charred New York strip smothered in mushrooms and green chile and named for James Patrick Dunigan, a regular customer who kept requesting green chile with his steak. So many customers started asking for it, she had to put it on the menu.

Rosalea's customers are legendary—artists John Sloan, Will Shuster, Randall Davey, Georgia O'Keeffe and Mark Rothko along with Oliver La Farge, Mabel Dodge Luhan, D.H.Lawrence's widow, Freda Lawrence, and even Harry Partch, the American composer and maker of exotic instruments, who washed dishes briefly here in exchange for room and board. There's a whole list of employees who are artists—Santa Fe painters, jewelers, photographers ... her friends.

Rosalea watches as couples and families arrive and are seated at tables in the crowded dining room. Tonight, some are local but many are out-of-towners, taking a break from driving to fuel up on her famous food, a blend of French Creole, Cajun, Spanish and standard American dishes spiced up with her own inspirations.

After hours, she brings out a bottle of vodka and something wonderful to eat, plays the records of Louis Armstrong and Fats Waller and has late-night discussions with friends and stragglers about art and life. There's always something to celebrate—the sale of a painting, a wedding, a birthday, a poetry reading. Once a month, she hosts art openings in the dining room, serving elegant molded mousses, some with seafood, served with crackers.

The Pink has been her life since she opened it in the summer of 1944, a brave move during wartime rationing of sugar and meat. Housed in a 300-year-old building in the heart of the historic Barrio de Analco, one of Santa Fe's oldest neighborhoods, The Pink sits just across the street from the San Miguel Mission, possibly the oldest church in America. The restaurant's building served as military barracks for Spanish soldiers and, according to legend, the main dining room served as quarters for Don Diego de Vargas when he was a Spanish commander under the viceroy of Spain. The walls are 36-inches thick and the six fireplaces come in handy during the winter months.

Rosalea moved to Santa Fe in 1938 shortly before the start of World War II. Encouraged to open a restaurant by friends who loved her cooking, she started The Pink when Santa Fe was still a sleepy town and you could buy firewood from the old men whose burros carried bundles of wood on their backs. She'd wanted to be an artist, but once she started the restaurant, her painting career was placed on the back burner.

She'd never cooked professionally before, but growing up in New Orleans she'd been influenced by the complex flavors of Creole and Cajun food. At The Pink, she serves food that is simple and honest—onion soup, hamburgers, apple pie—but also delicious and presented in the most tempting way possible. Her goal is to have her guests leave with a lasting, glowing memory.

At first the restaurant seated just 30 people and the menu was limited but everything was made with fresh, fine ingredients. The French onion soup and French apple pie were big hits, as was The 'Dobeburger—served with a delicious sauce made of mayonnaise, Worcestershire and Tabasco sauces, ketchup, garlic, savory and celery salt. It sold for 25 cents.

Later, she added chicken enchiladas with green chile and cheese, one of her favorite dishes on the menu. The Pink was the first restaurant to serve seafood in Santa Fe, and her lobster salad became famous. The Pink was also the first restaurant to use the elegant, local Nambé ware. Rosalea kept a stack of trademark oval bowls by the stove for serving. By her estimate, she's made thousands and thousands of her famous French apple pies served with hard sauce, all eaten with gusto.

Rosalea's New Orleans roots are visible in some of her dishes, including Shrimp Remoulade with Creole Mustard, Oysters St. Jacques, and of course, gumbo, the favorite soup of Louisiana. She's big on soups and stews because they smell so good while they're cooking and because no food is more nurturing than a bowlful of steaming soup. And while she's perfectly happy with a plate of cheese and a ripe pear for dessert, she had to

THE DRAGON ROOM

Rosalea Murphy's restaurant did so well that she opened the famous Dragon Room bar in 1978 on the spot where the patios were located, and it became famous for the drinks, camaraderie and the tree growing right up through the roof. It's so unique that *Newsweek International* named the Dragon Room one of the top 19 bars in the world.

While digging the foundations for the Dragon Room, workers uncovered the skull of a 13th-century native woman surrounded by pottery shards. After that, a woman dressed in brown is said to have begun haunting the bar, holding a lit candle and hovering near diners.

come up with desserts to satisfy her customers, so she added Creole Chocolate Cake and Flaming Sundae, ignited by a sugar cube soaked in lemon extract and placed on top of a marshmallow.

Oh, yes, Rosalea loves entertaining. The Pink's New Year's Eve party has become an annual tradition, and when the clock strikes midnight, balloons float down from the ceiling, and everybody blows whistles and kisses one another. Then, a bountiful buffet is served, with tamales, apricot-glazed ham and Southern black-eyed peas for good luck.

In fact, the entertaining aspect of her job is what she loves most—the theatricality, the people, the drama and the artistry required to make The Pink successful. And it *is* a resounding success judging by the crowds of diners. It's often hard to find a table in the dining room or on the two patios, where musicians play and an outdoor fireplace keeps the chill at bay.

Yes, Rosalea thinks, The Pink certainly has become a landmark, located on the famous Santa Fe Trail, where wagon trains once rumbled into town, headed for the Plaza down the street. That same road became Route 66, bringing weary travelers searching for a square meal to The Pink, as well as La Fonda, The Shed and the Plaza Café. This location sure has helped make her restaurant famous. That, and the good food.

When it opened, The Pink was the first fine dining establishment in the city, even though customers had to brown-bag their liquor because she had no liquor license. Now, people from around the world dine with her, and life is good.

Tonight, like every Friday night, it's bustling and there's a happy hum in the air. She looks around the room at the crowd savoring her cooking and feels sated. A waitress comes by with Rosalea's famous French apple pie and a little jug of hard sauce for the table. Suddenly, she's famished! She calls for more vodka, takes a big slice, sits back and soaks in the scene, happy to be out of the hot kitchen for a change.

THE MURPHY MARGARITA

SERVES 2

Margaritas, a big part of New Mexican cuisine, have long been a staple at The Pink. This simple recipe lets the main ingredients shine for a perfect blend of salty and sweet.

2 ounces gold tequila
1½ ounces Triple Sec
3 ounces bottled sweet and sour mix
1 ounce freshly squeezed lime juice
Salt
Lime, cut into wedges
Ice cubes

Fill a cocktail shaker with ice. Add the tequila, Triple Sec, sweet and sour mix and lime juice, and shake until mixed and chilled, about 30 seconds.

Rub the rims of two margarita glasses with lime wedges, and then dip into a bowl of salt to coat. Strain the margarita into the glasses and garnish with lime wedges.

SHRIMP REMOULADE

SERVES 4

Remoulade is a staple of Creole cuisine in Louisiana, where it's most often served with shrimp, but hard-boiled eggs were also popular since they were less expensive. Traditionally, the dish is paired with fried green tomatoes. For real authenticity, serve this in a Nambé dish, the way Rosalea did!

36 medium shrimp, raw
1 small clove garlic, peeled
8 whole allspice
6 peppercorns
½ teaspoon salt
Remoulade Sauce (see recipe below)
2 cups Romaine or other sturdy lettuce, shredded
½ cup fresh parsley, chopped
¼ cup black olives, chopped, for garnish
2 lemons, cut into wedges

Place the shrimp in a large saucepan and cover with water. Add the garlic, allspice, peppercorns and salt and slowly bring to a boil over medium heat. Let simmer until the shrimp turn pink, about 1 minute. Remove from the heat and let cool. Peel and devein the shrimp.

Remoulade Sauce:
2 tablespoons Creole mustard (see recipe below)
1 tablespoon tarragon-wine vinegar
¼ teaspoon salt
¼ teaspoon freshly ground pepper
1 cup olive oil
1 tablespoon paprika
½ cup celery, finely chopped
1 cup scallions, chopped
1 clove garlic, chopped

½ cup fresh parsley, chopped
2 tablespoons prepared horseradish
2 tablespoons anchovy paste, optional
Dash of cayenne pepper
2 tablespoons lemon juice, freshly squeezed
Tabasco sauce to taste

Combine the Creole mustard and vinegar in a large bowl, and season with salt and pepper. Gradually add the olive oil in a steady stream using a wire whisk, stirring constantly until the oil blends smoothly without any separation. Stir in the paprika, celery, scallions, garlic, parsley, horseradish, anchovy paste, cayenne pepper and lemon juice. Add Tabasco sauce to taste.

Place the shredded lettuce on four plates and scatter the shrimp on top. Cover with the Remoulade Sauce and marinate in the refrigerator for at least 1 hour (you'll get a better flavor if you leave it overnight). Serve garnished with the olives and lemon wedges.

Creole Mustard:
1 tablespoon Dijon mustard
1 tablespoon prepared horseradish
Tabasco sauce, to taste

Combine the mustard, horseradish and Tabasco sauce in a small bowl.

FRENCH ONION SOUP A LA PINK ADOBE

SERVES 4

Unlike traditional French onion soup, this recipe calls for Parmesan instead of Gruyère and croutons instead of baguette rounds, resulting in a refreshingly lighter version.

1 stick (8 tablespoons) butter
6 large white onions, peeled and sliced paper-thin
½ teaspoon sugar
¼ teaspoon fresh thyme, minced
3 quarts strong homemade or quality beef broth
¼ teaspoon salt
¼ teaspoon freshly ground black pepper
Homemade Croutons (see recipe below)
Freshly grated Parmesan cheese

Preheat oven to 450 degrees.

Melt the butter in a large pot over medium heat. Stir in the onions and keep stirring until they turn translucent. Add the sugar, thyme and beef broth, and simmer for 20 minutes. Season to taste with salt and pepper.

Place the croutons and Parmesan in pottery bowls and fill each with the soup. Sprinkle more Parmesan cheese on top. Place the bowls in the oven and bake until the cheese melts. Serve hot.

Homemade Croutons:
½ loaf day-old French bread, cubed
About ¼ cup olive oil
¼ teaspoon each: ground thyme, dried basil, dried rosemary, garlic salt and freshly ground black pepper

Preheat oven to 375 degrees.

Brush a tablespoon or two of olive oil on a baking sheet.

Combine bread cubes with remaining olive oil, herbs, salt and pepper in a large mixing bowl. Place on a baking sheet and bake until bread turns golden and crunchy, about 15 minutes.

AMERICA'S MOTHER ROAD

America's famous "Mother Road" stretched 2,448 miles across the country, passing through three time zones and eight states, and symbolizing freedom for American motorists in search of adventure and inspiration.

Inaugurated in 1926, Route 66 offered a moveable feast, with hotel restaurants and diners built along the way in an array of architectural styles, including Pueblo Revival, Spanish Colonial Revival, Southwest vernacular, Art Deco, and Neocolonial.

In New Mexico, Route 66 started as a 500-mile gravel road, made up of trails once used by wagon trains and railroads. It grew into a road linking Texas, New Mexico and Arizona, the largest stretch of Route 66 in all eight states. In 1936, a realignment moved the road away from Santa Fe but visitors continued to detour to the capital for its good food, its fine lodging, its art and its charm.

Other popular spots on the iconic highway in New Mexico included the Club Café in Santa Rosa, famous for its smiling Fat Man neon sign, and El Rancho Hotel in Gallup, built by film director D.W. Griffith's brother, R.E. Griffith, and frequented by Humphrey Bogart, John Wayne, James Stewart, Mae West, Katherine Hepburn, Spencer Tracy and other Hollywood stars.

ROUTE 66 BURGERS

SERVES 4

Burgers were on just about every menu along Route 66, from the classic cheeseburger to the New Mexico version, served with green chile. This recipe brings together the heat of green chile with the bite of blue cheese, a perfect combo.

1 pound ground round steak
¼ cup red onion, finely diced
¼ teaspoon salt
¼ teaspoon freshly ground black pepper
6 brioche buns, buttered and toasted
2 fresh, roasted New Mexico Hatch or Anaheim chile peppers,
    chopped (see Kitchen Clue, page 23)
4 thick slices blue cheese

Combine the ground round with the onions, salt and pepper in a medium bowl. Form into 4 patties and grill or broil to desired temperature, about 4 to 5 minutes per side for medium. Serve on lightly toasted brioche buns topped with green chile and cheese.

FRENCH LATTICE APPLE PIE

SERVES 8

The Pink's French Apple Pie was famous. This version incorporates a lattice crust and is topped with a hefty dollop of Cinnamon-Scented Whipped Cream.

Pie Crust (makes one 9-inch crust plus extra for lattice topping)
2 cups flour
½ teaspoon salt
12 tablespoons (1½ sticks) butter, chilled and cut into cubes
6-8 tablespoons ice water

Prepare the crust by combining the butter, flour and salt in a food processor until the mixture is crumbly. Add the ice water in a slow, steady stream while pulsing the mixture, until the dough begins to pull away from the sides of the mixing bowl. (You may also do all this in a bowl using a pastry cutter or fork to cut in the butter with the flour and salt. Slowly add the ice water, and continue to combine until the dough starts to pull away from the sides of the bowl.)

Turn the dough onto a lightly floured board and form into a ball. Cut into 4 quarters, and use the heel of your hand to smear each quarter, thoroughly mixing the butter into the dough. Roll the dough back into a ball, and press into a 6-inch circle, using your hands. Cover in plastic wrap and refrigerate 1 to 2 hours.

Remove the plastic wrap from the dough and roll out on a floured surface into a circle a bit larger than the size of your pie pan. Using the rolling pin, roll the dough up over the pin, and unroll into a 9-inch pie pan. Trim the extra crust around the edges and set extra dough aside.

Filling:
2 pounds, or 3 large Braeburn, Granny Smith, MacIntosh or other tart apples, peeled, cored and sliced
2 tablespoons lemon juice, freshly squeezed
½ teaspoon ground nutmeg
1 teaspoon vanilla extract
½ teaspoon ground cinnamon

2 tablespoons Vanilla Sugar
   (see Kitchen Clue, page 7)
½ cup raisins
½ cup brown sugar
2 tablespoons flour
2 tablespoons butter
½ cup pecans, coarsely chopped
1 egg white, lightly beaten

Preheat oven to 450 degrees.

Combine the apples, lemon juice, nutmeg, vanilla and cinnamon in a large bowl. Spoon the mixture into the unbaked pie crust and sprinkle evenly with Vanilla Sugar and raisins.

In a separate bowl, mix the brown sugar and flour. Cut in the butter with a pastry cutter or 2 knives until the mixture is crumbly. Spread over the entire pie. Sprinkle the top with the pecans.

Take the remaining pastry dough and roll out into a circle, about 1/4-inch thick. Using a knife, cut the pastry dough into 1-inch wide strips. Line the top of the pie with half the strips facing one way, then alternately weave the remaining strips the opposite way, carefully lifting the first row of strips to place the new strips underneath so you have a lattice crust top.

Brush the lattice crust with the egg white. Bake for 10 minutes, and then reduce heat to 350 and bake an additional 30 minutes. Serve warm with Cinnamon-Scented Whipped Cream (see page 38).

GOING OUT IN STYLE

Rosalea Murphy passed away in 2000 at age 88, and was buried in her famous "R" and "M" earrings made by Santa Fe artist Doug Magnus and her custom boots, hand-tooled with her famous rooster imagery by Scott Wayne. Her family continued to run The Pink until 2008, when it was sold.

CHAPTER TEN

GEORGIA O'KEEFFE, LEGEND IN ABIQUIÚ

(1960s)

"It was all so far away—there was quiet and an
untouched feel to the country and I could work as I pleased."

GEORGIA O'KEEFFE

HIGH SUMMER IN NORTHERN NEW MEXICO AND GEORGIA O'KEEFFE IS UP WITH THE dawn, her dogs sitting by the fire as she sips tea in bed and watches the sunrise. Morning is the best time—no people around. Soon, she'll get up, take a walk, have breakfast—maybe scrambled or soft-boiled eggs with toast and a savory jam, green chile with garlic and oil, sliced fresh fruit and strong coffee.

She'll work all morning in her studio, stopping only for the noon meal, usually a salad with herbs and lettuce from the garden. Probably another walk just before supper, leaving ample time for an evening drive through the landscape she's painted so many times.

When she isn't in her studio, Georgia's in the garden, coaxing turnips, lettuce, carrots, beets, cucumbers, squash and corn from the soil. She also grows beans, onions and garlic, tomatoes, green chile, cabbage, broccoli, bell peppers and marigolds, strategically placed to keep away insects. Herbs include tarragon, dill, green and purple basil, lovage, marjoram, sorrel, parsley, savory and three kinds of mint. And the flowers! Grape hyacinths, daffodils and crocuses. Lilacs, irises, columbines, roses, poppies. Fruit trees include pear, apple and apricot, and there are mulberry and raspberry bushes, too.

Georgia grows three varieties of apples, carefully wrapping them in paper for storage. Her yellow apples—plucked just before ripening—make the best applesauce in the world. She likes to serve apples sliced, with thin slices of *geitost* (caramelized goat milk), or to make her Norwegian spiced apple cake with rum sauce.

The garden was the primary reason she bought the property. She first saw the house while spending the summer on a dude ranch near Alcalde. Perched up high and isolated from the tiny village, the hacienda was vacant, one tree collapsed over a wall. But there was a garden and a patio with a large door in one wall that, when opened, revealed a white pig standing inside! Right then and there, Georgia knew she had to have the house, the same way she knew that if she painted Pedernal Mountain enough, she could have that, too.

But the house wasn't for sale. It was uninhabitable and took her 15 years to work out a plan with the church that owned it to buy the place for $10—about the value of the house when it had first sold, according to the original deed, in a trade for some corn, a cow and a serape. Georgia then spent the next four years renovating the place, with the help of her friend, Maria Chabot.

Georgia's artistry can be seen in the care she takes with her food. When the apricots ripen, she dries them on large screens outside and later adds them to muffins and waffles. She hangs bunches of herbs from the vigas in the Indian Room, a dark, cool room a few steps down and off from the kitchen. It is called the "Indian Room" because its narrow adobe ledges—used to store roasted green chile, frozen corn, lamb's quarter, green peaches, raspberries and her famous applesauce—resemble beds used by early Pueblo people. Georgia also has a pantry filled with canned and dried produce from the garden, some commercially canned items and spices and grains.

Georgia prefers organic grains and she makes her own bread, grinding the flour in a small mill. She browns the bread in her old-fashioned toaster for breakfast, served with eggs and honey purchased from her neighbors. She likes to buy good black bread and fine cheese from Bode's General Merchandise, on the main road into Abiquiú.

With most meals, Georgia serves soup. She finds it such a comfort. She usually eats it with a salad and vegetable and bread or crackers, followed by dessert. Sometimes a friend will bring her a gift of wild asparagus, which grows abundantly nearby. She likes to steam vegetables and serve them with a dab of butter, oil and herb salt. She could eat spinach with every meal. Eggs Florentine, a poached egg on a bed of spinach, is a favorite.

Once a week or so, she enjoys a thick, juicy steak, usually for lunch and ordered from a Santa Fe market. For holidays, she serves a roast leg of lamb with garlic, honey mint sauce, mashed potatoes with dandelion greens, steamed carrots and white fruitcake. On Christmas Eve, she puts out *farolitos* (paper bags filled with sand and a burning votive candle) and serves traditional tamales, empanaditas and posole.

After dinner, she listens to Beethoven and Bach, Gregorian chants and the early music of Monteverdi. Before going to bed, she reads. Cookbooks provide such pleasant nighttime company, but she also enjoys Kakuzo Okakura's *The Book of Tea*.

Georgia's kitchen is an extension of her self—simple and utilitarian. It overlooks her ornamental cherry trees and the Chama River Valley. A worktable near the stove is covered with a red-and-white checkered tablecloth. Pots and pans hang from one white wall and mixing bowls, whisks, beaters and graters from another. When she's cooking, she'll tie on her apron, trimmed with rick rack in three colors.

The dining room has a white-stained plywood table, a few cushioned, straight-backed chairs draped with Mexican weavings and an eternal arrangement of irises or lilacs. There's a corner fireplace, long windows covered with white muslin curtains and an African sculpture on one wall. On another, a nicho showcases a statue of Guan Yim, Buddhist goddess of mercy and compassion, and the smooth black river rocks she collects on her walks. Georgia likes to serve meals on plain white china with simple stainless steel flatware, white fringed napkins and straw placemats.

As much as she loves her Abiquiú house, Georgia also enjoys spending time in the first house she bought in New Mexico, Los Rancho de los Burros—a simple cabin on Ghost Ranch, a 21,000-acre dude ranch surrounded by endless skies and stark beauty. The place symbolizes a kind of freedom to her, isolated as it is from the world with no telephone and electricity provided only by a generator. It's the perfect place for an artist to really dig in and work...

Georgia has always wanted to be an artist. She took art lessons at home, on the family farm in Sun Prairie, Wisconsin where she grew up the second of seven children. (She was named for her maternal grandfather, George Victor Totto, a Hungarian count.) Georgia later studied at The Art Institute of Chicago and at the Art Students League of New York when imitative realism was in vogue. Her "Untitled" painting of a dead rabbit with copper pot won the league's William Merritt Chase still-life prize in 1908, earning her a spot at the school's outdoor summer school in Lake George, N.Y.

When she was offered a teaching position in the public schools in Amarillo, Texas, Georgia went straightaway. And why not? She'd been captivated by the Wild West since she was a child, when her mother read her stories about Kit Carson and Billy the Kid. A few years later, she attended Columbia University Teachers College to study with Arthur Wesley Dow, a leader of the American Arts & Crafts Movement whom she greatly admired.

It was a Columbia classmate who showed Georgia's drawings to photographer and gallery owner Alfred Stieglitz. He told Georgia they were the purest, finest, sincerest things he had seen in a long while and presented her first solo show, which opened April 3, 1917, at his New York gallery, 291. There she met the famous Mabel Dodge Luhan from Taos.

Georgia and Stieglitz eventually married, but over the years, she'd grown tired of summers with the Stieglitz family at Lake George in upstate New York. Seeking new inspiration for her work, she'd weighed a few options for the summer of 1929: rent a separate studio in Lake George, travel to Europe or visit Santa Fe? Having first seen New Mexico in 1917 and remembering its stark beauty, she'd decided on the latter.

She'd taken the train to Santa Fe and then visited Taos at the invitation of Mabel, who even provided Georgia with her own studio. She went on pack trips and visited D.H. Lawrence at his ranch in San Cristobal, where she painted "The Lawrence Tree." She'd also painted the Ranchos de Taos church, Penitente crosses and other regional subjects. Inspired by the mystical landscape, Georgia came to call New Mexico "the faraway." After this trip, she realized she could never live anywhere else.

And so she'd begun spending part of nearly every year at Ghost Ranch and bought the tiny cabin on the property in 1940. Stieglitz, on the other hand, rarely left New York and not once ventured to New Mexico for a visit. Though they remained married until his death in 1946, their relationship was strained by distance and his infidelity. After his death, Georgia moved permanently to the land of blue skies, and never looked back.

She bought a Model A Ford and outfitted it for painting. The high windows let in plenty of light, and after unbolting the driver's seat, she can turn it around and paint with her canvas propped up on the back seat. She takes the car on camping trips with her friend Maria, often to the Black Place, an isolated spot in the Bisti Badlands of Navajo country. During the day, she sketches, draws and takes photographs. At sunset, they eat dinner,—pieces of venison wrapped in bacon and cooked in a long-handled toaster over the fire. They sleep in a tent and rise early for a breakfast of oatmeal and another day of work.

And now the sun is rising on this new day and it's time to get going, out to the light, to the red rocks and to the mesas. Out for a walk in the desert. Georgia shakes her head from her reverie, places the empty teacup on the bedside table and calls for the dogs.

ICONIC ARTIST

Georgia O'Keeffe, one of the world's most famous artists, lived from 1887 to 1986. Until failing eyesight forced her to stop painting in 1984, she worked in pencil and watercolor and clay. After she died, her ashes were scattered at the top of her beloved Pedernal Mountain. Her home and studio in Abiquiú were designated a National Historic Landmark, and the U.S. Post Office issued a 32-cent stamp honoring her. A fossilized species of a Triassic reptile discovered on the grounds of Ghost Ranch, was named *Effigia okeeffeae* in her honor. O'Keeffe's painting "Jimson Weed" set a new auction record for the most expensive work of art by a woman when it sold for $44.4 million in 2014.

ABIQUIÚ APPLESAUCE

MAKES ABOUT 4 CUPS

This simple recipe is inspired by one Georgia O'Keeffe used to make with her home-grown apples. She was very proud of her applesauce. This recipe combines tart and sweet apples with cinnamon and vanilla and it's perfect with ice cream, pies, potato pancakes and other dishes.

3 pounds tart and sweet Braeburn, Granny Smith or Macintosh apples,
    peeled, cored and quartered
2 tablespoons Vanilla Sugar (see Kitchen Clue, page 7)
2 tablespoons lemon juice, freshly squeezed
½ teaspoon vanilla extract
½ teaspoon ground cinnamon, for garnish

Place the apples in a large pot filled with about 2 cups of water. Bring the water to a boil, reduce the heat and simmer until the apples turn soft, about 40 minutes. Cool, and then transfer the apples to a food processor and process until smooth. Stir in the sugar, lemon juice and vanilla. Serve warm, sprinkled with the cinnamon.

WATERCRESS EGG DROP SOUP

SERVES 2

This lovely, light soup has Asian notes, with threads of cooked egg, chicken broth and the spice of watercress. Serve it for lunch or dinner, paired with a garden salad.

1 bunch fresh watercress (about 6 ounces)
4 cups homemade chicken broth
2 eggs, room temperature
¼ teaspoon salt
¼ teaspoon freshly ground black pepper
Sour cream, for garnish

Clean and chop the watercress into 1-inch lengths, discarding the tough stems. Heat the broth in a medium saucepan over medium heat.

Break the eggs into a bowl and beat lightly with a fork. When the broth is simmering, toss in the watercress, lower the heat, and slowly add the eggs in a thin stream, letting them cook quickly in delicate threads. Remove from heat, and add salt and pepper. Serve hot, with a dollop of sour cream.

CURRIED CHICKEN

SERVES 2-4

This version of an O'Keeffe favorite is complex and flavorful, with curry powder, tart apples, raisins and balsamic vinegar. It's delicious, hot or cold—as an entree with rice or as a salad or sandwich.

2 tablespoons butter

1 large shallot, peeled and sliced

1 large Braeburn, Granny Smith, Macintosh or other tart apple, cored,
    peeled and diced

1 tablespoon all-purpose flour

1 cup milk

1½ cup white chicken meat, cooked and cut into chunks

1 teaspoon Dijon mustard

¼ cup dark raisins

2 teaspoons curry powder, or to taste

1 teaspoon balsamic vinegar

¼ teaspoon salt

¼ teaspoon freshly ground black pepper

Melt 1 tablespoon of the butter in a large saucepan over medium heat. Add the shallots and apples and cook for about 10 minutes, stirring occasionally, until apples turn soft, about ten minutes. Transfer to another dish and set aside.

Wipe out the pan, then use it to make a roux, melting the second tablespoon of butter and whisking in the flour. Slowly add the milk, whisking continuously, until the mixture thickens and bubbles. Stir in the apple mixture, chicken, mustard, raisins and curry, and simmer for 5 to 10 minutes, until hot.

Remove the pan from the heat and whisk in the balsamic vinegar. Season with salt and pepper and serve.

ZABAGLIONE

SERVES 2

A traditional Italian dessert, light and frothy, enjoyed by Georgia O'Keeffe on dark winter evenings.

3 egg yolks
2 tablespoons sugar
½ cup marsala, port or sherry
Ground nutmeg, for garnish

Heat water to a simmer in a double boiler. Place the egg yolks in top of the double boiler and add the sugar, beating until thick and lemon-colored. Set well above the simmering water and slowly add the wine, whisking until the mixture becomes light, smooth and slightly firm. Spoon into dessert cups or glasses, and sprinkle with ground nutmeg. Serve immediately or chill and serve later, accompanied by ladyfingers, if desired.

CHAPTER ELEVEN

DENNIS HOPPER, MUD PALACE MOVIE STAR

(1970s)

"Taos, man. Taos, N.M. There's freedom there.
They don't mind long hair. The herds mingle."

DENNIS HOPPER

IT'S 2 A.M. AND DENNIS HOPPER IS WIDE AWAKE AND STONED OUT OF HIS MIND. Wrapped in a coat made from a Navajo blanket, his trademark hairband over his long brown hair, he's sitting crossed legged on the floor of the Rainbow Room in the Mud Palace in Taos, listening to Dylan's new album, a near-empty bottle of rum at his side.

He still can't believe he owns this eccentric estate built by the woman who introduced Taos to the world. Dennis has plans to follow in the footsteps of Mabel Dodge Luhan, creating a utopia for his counterculture friends, maybe even a new center for Hollywood—the *authentic* Hollywood. And the Mud Palace—man, the Palace!—will be at the center of it all, his spiritual home … his *heart* home.

Dennis stumbled upon Mabel's rambling estate in 1968 during a scouting trip for *Easy Rider*, the movie he co-authored, directed, starred in and edited. When it opened, the film that had cost just $400,000 to make earned a quick $20 million. (Thank God they'd ditched the film's original and forgettable title, *The Loner*.) Two years later, in March 1970, Dennis used some of his earnings to buy Mabel's house, with its original furnishings from the old lady's granddaughter for $160,000.

And Mabel's furnishings are far out! He's surrounded by luxurious couches, Italian silk fabrics and wooden beams painted to resemble an Indian blanket. But in place of Mabel's modernist paintings, Dennis has hung his own collection of works by Andy Warhol, Jasper Johns, Ed Ruscha, Roy Lichtenstein and Robert Rauschenberg. His folk art collection is displayed too—*retablos, santos*, Peruvian masks and a ghostly Penitente death cart, which he claims follows him around the house at times.

In fact, the whole house spooks the hell out of him sometimes. Mabel wrote her memoirs in the Rainbow Room, where he can feel her creative spirit. He sleeps upstairs in her master bedroom, in a groovy white bed, hand-carved with spiral twists by a Taos Pueblo guy. He's heard that Mabel's servants used white shoe polish to hide the scuffs. When the wind howls, he swears he can hear the sound of drumming and singing from the ghost of Mabel's husband, Taos Pueblo chief, Tony Lujan.

Dennis spent many long months in the Mud Palace editing *The Last Movie*. He bought the old Taos cinema, El Cortez—across from the Ranchos de Taos church—to screen his opus, and the screenings lasted as long as eight hours. Later, the film that was supposed to have been his masterpiece, bombed with both critics and audiences when it opened, and was quickly pulled from theaters. So he's been holed up in Taos, hiding away from Hollywood.

It's the perfect party house, and Dennis throws regular fiestas with all the hip cats—Bob Dylan, John Wayne, Leonard Cohen, the Everly Brothers, Peter Fonda, Jack Nicholson, Dean Stockwell, Kris Kristofferson and tons of hippies. Booze and drugs are served with generosity at dinners around a big table, like a twisted version of *The Last Supper*. When he needs to get out of the house for some real food, he'll head over to El Patio just off the Plaza for green chile stew and tamales, or to Ranchos Plaza Grill for their huevos rancheros. Sometimes he'll take a gang down the road to the Old Martinez Dance Hall to eat green chile chicken enchiladas and dance all night to live music on the bouncy wooden floors. Or he'll just hang out at the Sagebrush Inn, drinking Coors.

If Dennis has a favorite room in the Mud Palace, it's the solarium, with views of mystical Taos Mountain and its sacred Blue Lake. From there, you can also see the *morada*, the church of the Penitentes, where secret rituals take place that date back centuries. The solarium is where he married Michelle Phillips

THE LAST MOVIE

The inspiration for *The Last Movie* came to Dennis Hopper in Durango, Mexico, when he was on set for the John Wayne movie, *The Sons of Katie Elder*. He started wondering what happened when a Hollywood movie shooting in an exotic location ended, and left the natives living among the discarded sets.

He'd been ready to start filming in 1966 but music producer Phil Spector reneged on the financial support he'd promised, even after Dennis cast Spector as a cocaine dealer in *Easy Rider*. Following the success of *Easy Rider*, Universal Studios gave him $850,000 and total control over the film as long as he stayed on budget.

Shot in the Peruvian Andes, *The Last Movie* tells the story of a stunt man who stays behind after production of a Hollywood Western wraps. Hopper saw it as a story about how America was destroying itself.

The cast and crew spent two weeks in Cuzco, staying in a European hotel that served tea and cakes every day at 4 p.m., but most people involved with the movie went straight to the bar to drink Pisco Sours, a whiskey sour-style drink made with distilled grapes. In their free time, they played poker. And in his drug-addled, booze-soaked state, Dennis shot a record-setting quarter of a million feet of film. While *The Last Movie* won the Critics' Prize at the Venice Film Festival, American viewers hated it.

(of The Mamas & the Papas) on Halloween in 1970, with 200 guests crammed into the room, lit by hundreds of candles that almost burned the damn house down. Eight days later, she filed for divorce. She says she left him because of his unnatural sexual demands but won't elaborate to the press. Well, then, he won't talk about it either. But it did involve handcuffs and it wasn't until the eighth day that things turned bad...

He'd met Michelle while she was dating Jack Nicholson. She had tested for a role in *Carnal Knowledge* but lost out to Candice Bergen. So she'd signed on to play the female lead in *The Last Movie* instead, making her film debut. She'd flown to Peru to work on location and they'd fallen crazy-in-love. She said her "Florence Nightingale" need to save people is what drew her to him. It was easy to see what drew him to her. Just look at her, man! So they'd come to Taos and gotten hitched, with Michelle's friend, Ann Marshall, and Don Everly of the Everly Brothers as witnesses. Don brought the marriage license to make it official.

Taos with Michelle was a trip! She had touched up the windows in the upstairs bathroom, windows originally painted by D.H. Lawrence, when he'd spent time at Mabel's. Ironically, the author of the highly censored novel, *Lady Chatterley's Lover*, was so scandalized by those transparent windows that he'd painted them with colorful peacocks, flowers and other imagery to prevent anyone from seeing inside. The bathroom was also the setting for a scene in *American Dreamer* (the documentary about him)—he's in the bathtub with two Playboy bunnies.

If only he'd had the Mud Palace to use as a setting in *Easy Rider*. But they'd done all right. Dennis was the first person allowed to film on Taos Pueblo and they'd also shot on location at Manby Hot Springs. They wanted to film on location at New Buffalo, one of 27 communes near Taos, but they couldn't get permission so they re-created the commune as a movie set in L.A., in a spot overlooking Malibu Canyon. Peter Fonda's kids—four-year-old Bridget and her younger brother, Justin—were cast as hippie commune children.

In one of Hopper's favorite *Easy Rider* scenes, filmed at the Taos jail, Jack Nicholson's character, George Hanson, walks away from a stint in the drunk tank. He takes a swig from a bottle of Jack Daniels and makes a toast: "Here's the first of the day, fellas! To old D.H. Lawrence!" Hopper loves this line because he's a huge fan of Lawrence. Man, he was authentic ... the "first freak!" The guy who fueled Dennis's own vision of Taos as an alternative Hollywood, a film-making center much like the utopia Lawrence had hoped to create here.

The night before filming that scene, he and Jack dropped acid at the top of Lobo Mountain on Lawrence's ranch. Dennis wanted to do for film what Lawrence had done for literature. But now, with the bad reviews of *The Last Movie*, the Mud Palace has become more of a retreat, the center of nothing at all. He's been branded as the *enfant terrible* of Hollywood and blacklisted from movies because of his alcohol and drug-fueled tirades on set.

So let Hollywood come to him! He throws his parties and the cool people show up. Sometimes he gets so drunk and high that he shoots his gun at the walls. He's got some anger issues, all right. He's fighting with Peter Fonda about the rights to the majority of the residual profits on *Easy Rider*. He's pissed that Hollywood's kicked him out. He's stunned that *The Last Movie* flopped, and don't get him started on Michelle...

When people ask why he's living at the end of the world, he tells them it's because he doesn't like the people in Los Angeles, even though they do have nice banks. "I tell you, man," he says, "you ought to come down here to Taos. It's beautiful. Taos is the beautiful place to be." Yet, there are those days when he comes downstairs in the morning for orange juice and finds some 30 hippies hanging out in his kitchen. "Who are *you*?" someone always asks him.

But Dennis is not down and out. Not yet. He believes in living to the edge of your senses. Just look at his early idols, all drug addicts and alcoholics—Arthur Rimbaud, Edmund Kean, John Barrymore—and he was friends with comedian Lenny Bruce before he overdosed. His career has been fueled by such extremes. After all, it was Natalie Wood who'd seduced him when he was 18 on the set of *Rebel Without a Cause*. Later, he married Brooke Hayward, daughter of legendary Broadway producer Leland Hayward, against her father's wishes. He still remembers Brooke's father following them up the aisle at the wedding, whispering in her ear, "Still not too late to get out of it." Brooke's best friend, Jane Fonda, hosted their wedding reception in her New York apartment, and that's where Dennis met Peter, over sandwiches and drinks.

There was a time, over in Malibu, when they'd all get together for Sunday lunches of Jane's excellent bouillabaisse and French garlic bread at the big farm table with her husband at the time, French film director Roger Vadim.

It was Brooke who had surprised Dennis with a Nikon camera because he was always framing pictures with his hands, wherever he went. The marriage lasted eight years, but his relationship with that camera made him famous! Portraits of Martin Luther King marches, Andy Warhol, Jane Fonda and the cover art he made for Ike and Tina Turner's single, *River Deep-Mountain High*. That was back when he'd started collecting art. He was one of the first people to buy an Andy Warhol Campbell's Soup print (for just $75!). He bought that print in 1962, the day his daughter, Marin, was born. And then he'd thrown a big party for Andy at their house, with chili and hot dogs served from a hot dog stand.

Chili and hot dogs ... just thinking about those hot dogs makes Dennis hungry. He notices that he's no longer sitting in darkness and night has given way to early dawn. He hauls himself up and heads upstairs to the solarium to catch the sunrise. Then he'll rustle up some eggs, bacon and coffee and try to greet the day. *Right on!* Hopefully there won't be any strangers leftover from last night's party in his kitchen.

HUEVOS RANCHEROS

SERVES 2

Huevos Rancheros, or "Rancher's Eggs," is a classic New Mexico breakfast dish made with eggs cooked in the traditional style of mid-morning meals served on rural farms in Mexico. The dish is often served with guacamole, Spanish rice or refried beans.

Red Chile Sauce:
2 tablespoons olive oil
3 cloves garlic, minced
½ cup chile powder, preferably Chimayó
2 cups beef broth
¼ teaspoon salt
¼ teaspoon freshly ground black pepper

Heat the olive oil in a medium saucepan over medium heat. Add the garlic and cook for 1 minute, until sizzling. Stir in the chile powder and beef broth and simmer until the sauce thickens, stirring occasionally, about 15 minutes. Season with salt and pepper. Use immediately or store in the refrigerator for up to a week.

Eggs:
1-2 tablespoons olive oil
4 small corn tortillas
4 eggs
About ¼ cup lettuce, shredded
1 large tomato, chopped
½ onion, diced (for garnish)
4 tablespoons Monterey Jack cheese, grated

Heat 1 tablespoon of the oil in a large frying pan over medium heat and, using tongs, place the tortillas in the pan and cook for just a few minutes on each side, until soft. You may need to add more oil after cooking each tortilla. Drain on paper towels.

Fry the eggs sunny side up. Place one cooked egg on top of each tortilla, drape with the red chile sauce and top with the lettuce, tomato, onion and cheese.

TAOS TENDERLOIN

SERVES 4

This recipe was inspired by a dish served at an event for Dennis Hopper, who proclaimed it the best tenderloin he'd ever tasted. The mushroom and marsala sauce makes this an especially rich entree.

1 3-4 pound beef tenderloin
½ teaspoon salt
½ teaspoon freshly ground pepper
4 tablespoons butter, at room temperature
2 large garlic cloves, minced
1 tablespoon fresh thyme, chopped
1 tablespoon fresh rosemary, chopped
1 tablespoon fresh sage, chopped
¼ teaspoon paprika

Preheat oven to 400 degrees.

Rub the tenderloin on all sides with salt and pepper. Place a large pan over high heat, and sear tenderloin on all sides until nicely browned, about 10 minutes total. Remove from heat and let cool.

Combine the butter, garlic, thyme, rosemary, sage and paprika in a small bowl and rub the mixture on the top side of the tenderloin. Place, top side up, in a baking pan and roast for about 30 minutes for medium rare, or until a meat thermometer inserted in the middle reads 130 degrees. Remove from the oven, and tent with aluminum foil and let cool for 20 minutes.

Mushroom Gravy:
2 tablespoons butter
1 cup wild mushrooms, cremini, or baby portobellos, sliced
2 shallots, thinly sliced
3 large cloves garlic, minced
¼ cup all-purpose flour
¼ cup Marsala

1 cup vegetable broth

¼ cup heavy cream

¼ teaspoon salt

¼ teaspoon freshly ground pepper

¼ teaspoon paprika

Heat the butter in a large pan over medium heat. Add the mushrooms and shallots and cook until mushrooms soften, about 5 minutes. Stir in garlic and cook for about 1 minute. Whisk in the flour to coat the mushrooms and let cook until the flour starts to brown. Stir in the Marsala and cook until reduced, about 1 minute. Slowly whisk in the broth, bring to a boil and cook, stirring frequently, until sauce thickens. Remove from heat. Season with salt, pepper and paprika.

TAMALEWOOD

Dennis Hopper joins a long list of movie makers who have filmed in New Mexico, including Thomas Edison, who took the train from New Jersey to Albuquerque in 1898 and shot *Indian Day School*. The 50-second film shows a group of Pueblo children and their teacher filing out of a schoolhouse on Isleta Pueblo. In 1912, D.W. Griffith visited Albuquerque and shot *Pueblo Legend*, a love story starring Mary Pickford as a Hopi maiden with a Pueblo boyfriend. Over the decades the Land of Enchantment has starred in numerous films and television series including *The Grapes of Wrath, The Man from Laramie, Billy Jack, Journey to the Center of the Earth, No Country for Old Men* and the hit cable series *Breaking Bad*.

THE LAST MOVIE'S PISCO SOURS

SERVES 1

Pisco, created by Spanish settlers in the 16th century, is made out of grape wine from the winemaking regions of Peru and Chile. It has a smooth flavor and the alcohol is hard to taste, leading many first-time tasters to not notice its effects. It's so popular in Peru that people celebrate Pisco Sour Day on the first Saturday of February every year.

1 egg white
2½ ounces Pisco Capel
½ ounce simple syrup (see Kitchen Clue)
¾ ounce lemon juice, freshly squeezed
Angostura Bitters

Fill a cocktail shaker with ice. Add all of the ingredients except the bitters and shake vigorously for 15 seconds. Strain into a chilled cocktail glass and top with a few drops of the bitters.

KITCHEN CLUE

Simple syrup is basically liquefied sugar used to sweeten cocktails and other beverages because it blends easier with cold drinks than regular sugar does. The recipe is a cinch: bring 1 cup of sugar and 1 cup of water to a boil in a small saucepan and simmer for about 3 minutes, until the sugar is dissolved. Remove from the heat and let cool completely. You can refrigerate this in a glass jar for up to a month.

MUD PALACE BROWNIES

MAKES ABOUT A DOZEN BROWNIES

These are just good old-fashioned brownies, spiced with red chile, though the Mud Palace version may have included a certain controlled substance purported to go well with chocolate. These go well with whipped cream.

2 ounces semisweet chocolate, preferably Baker's
½ cup (1 stick) butter
½ teaspoon ground cinnamon
½ teaspoon chile powder
2 eggs
1 cup Vanilla Sugar (see Kitchen Clue, page 7)
¾ cup all-purpose flour
½ cup pecans, roughly chopped

Preheat oven to 350 degrees. Butter and flour a 9x13-inch baking pan.

Bring 3 inches of water to a boil in a large saucepan then lower to a simmer. Place a smaller saucepan in the simmering water, add the chocolate and butter and remove from the heat. Let sit for about 10 minutes, until the mixture has melted. Stir until combined. Add the cinnamon and chile powder, and let cool.

Beat the eggs and sugar in a medium bowl with a whisk until thick. Fold the chocolate-butter mixture into the egg mixture and combine well. Gently fold the flour into the batter, and then stir in pecans.

Pour the batter into the prepared baking pan and bake until set, about 30 minutes. Cool on a wire rack. Cut into squares and serve.

DENNIS HOPPER'S LONG RIDE

Dennis Hopper sold his Mud Palace in 1978, but stayed in Taos until 1984, renting the Tony House nearby, where Tony Lujan had often stayed. He had hallucinations of Lawrence's ghost wandering the patio and when his guests overindulged, Mabel's ghost reportedly knocked paintings off the wall and onto their heads. But more frightening was the hostility that developed between the residents of the Mud Palace and the locals, who felt threatened by the invasion of hippies. The palace became an armed camp and Hopper, who carried a gun everywhere, was thrown in the Taos jail multiple times.

"I think of Taos as my home," Hopper told *The New Yorker* in 1971. "Taos Mountain is one of the sacred seven. And there's the sacred Blue Lake. If you drilled straight through...you'd come to Tibet...People come into Taos, have a flat tire, and stay the rest of their lives—or they can't wait to get out! It drives some people crazy."

After Taos, Hopper lived in Venice Beach in a mansion designed by Frank Gehry that was filled from floor to ceiling with his art collection. He was nominated for two Oscars and earned a star on the Hollywood Walk of Fame in 2010.

He died on May 20, 2010, from cancer, and was buried in a simple plot in Taos as a band of Hells Angels gunned their engines in loving tribute. New Mexico Governor Bill Richardson declared his birthday, May 17, as Dennis Hopper Day in New Mexico and Taos hosts an annual Dennis Hopper Day celebration with rides along "Hopper Highway," which retraces the route taken by the *Easy Rider* characters.

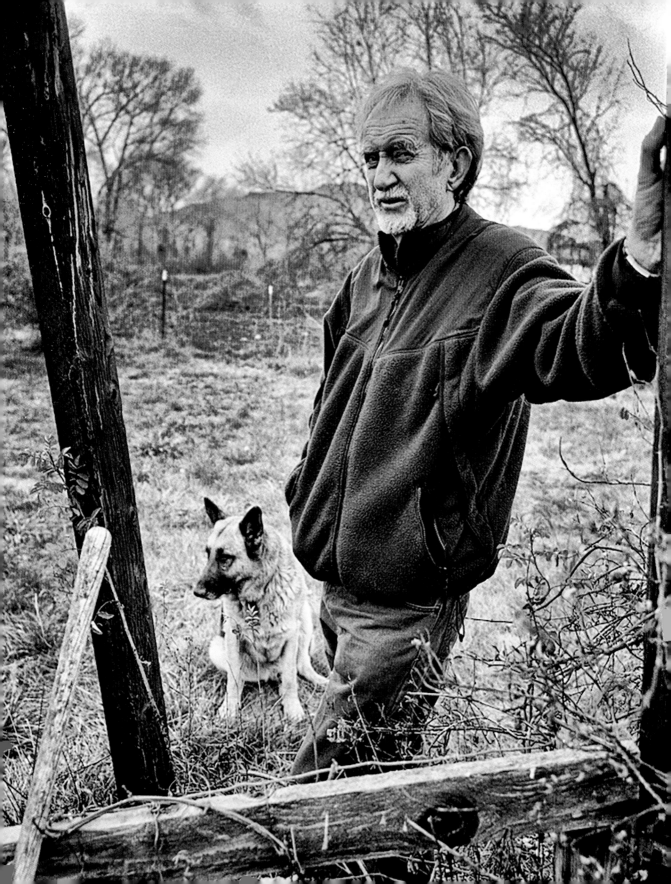

CHAPTER TWELVE

STANLEY CRAWFORD, THE GARLIC KING

(2015)

*"...to dream a garden and then to plant it is an act of independence
and even defiance to the greater world."*

STANLEY CRAWFORD

SATURDAY MORNING AT THE END OF HARVEST SEASON AND STAN CRAWFORD IS AT THE Santa Fe Farmers' Market, weighing bulbs of Russian Red and Bosque Early garlic for customers, sharing family news, recipes and cooking tips. He's surrounded by other farmers who also got up before dawn to drive here from places all across northern New Mexico and sell their fresh produce, their organic meat and poultry, their salsas, jams, eggs, cheese, bread and lavender.

The crowds are thick this morning under a brilliant blue sky. According to *USA Today* and numerous other publications, the Santa Fe Farmers' Market is one of the top in the country, and harvest time is always the busiest. Stan's been coming here since the early 1970s. He's sold at the markets in Taos, Española and Los Alamos, but Santa Fe is by far the biggest. Each weekend, he and his wife, RoseMary, make the hour drive south, from their farm in the small town of Dixon. Their truck is filled with garlic, shallots, cipollinis, kale, chard, turnips, beets, carrots, arugula, spinach, winter squash and New England pie pumpkins. They also have Skyphos, Oscarde and Adriana lettuce, all grown at El Bosque Garlic Farm.

Nestled in the foothills of the Rockies, the farm takes its name from the

Spanish word for "forest." The Embudo River, a rocky tributary of the Rio Grande, runs nearby. When Stan and RoseMary first saw the *acequia* (irrigation ditch), they were intrigued by the paradox of a waterway in the desert, a waterway constructed by Spanish settlers in the 18th century. Even the trees on this property had a history: the *Manzana Mexicana*, or Mexican apple, was brought to the region from Central Asia via Spain, much like the route garlic traveled to get here. They decided to buy the two acres for $2,300 and put down roots.

Stan, too, traveled the globe before landing in New Mexico. He grew up in a San Diego suburb where everyone had chickens, rabbits and fruit trees. His father, a high school shop teacher, kept an acre of avocado and citrus trees. Stan went on to study at the University of Chicago, the Sorbonne and the University of California at Berkeley, where he decided to try his hand at writing fiction. He journeyed to Greece, living for a time on Lesbos and Crete among expatriate writers, including William Golding, author of *Lord of the Flies.*

On Lesbos, Stan wrote his first novel, *Gascoyne,* an absurdist story about a man who drove around Los Angeles conducting business from his car via phone. Later, he sold the movie rights for $35,000. On Crete, he wrote a second novel, *Travel Notes,* and met RoseMary, who had worked as an Australian reporter for the *Daily Telegraph* in Sydney and as a publicist in London, wooing clients such as Marlon Brando and Frank Sinatra with drinks and dinner at the Savoy. Stan and RoseMary married in Athens and then moved to Dublin, where their son, Adam, was born.

Eventually they made their way to San Francisco, only to find a turbulent city rocked by anti-war protests and civil rights movements. So they traded in the Mercedes Stan had bought with the money from the movie rights for a VW camper and moved to New Mexico in search of a better place to raise a family. They were following friends, galvanized by Dennis Hopper's *Easy Rider* and its obvious message to "Head for the hills!" The land portrayed was so exotic, many Americans thought it was still a part of Mexico.

In the spirit of the times, Stan and RoseMary bought their two acres and planted a garden. Later, they expanded into full-fledged farming. Like many of their neighbors, they grew their own food, built their own house, dug ditches and mended fences. Their daughter, Kate, was born in New Mexico and she and her brother grew up on tofu, bean sprouts and homemade whole grain bread—sometimes longing for white bread, salami, and other "normal" foods.

It was a neighbor who brought Stan his first garlic bulbs, which had been growing wild in his orchard. Stan planted them that spring, using a hoe to dig a trench in soft soil. He dropped the cloves in, covered them with dirt and tamped down the soil. He relied on advice from plant encyclopedias but the green stems withered by midsummer and the bulbs he dug up were tiny, and hadn't even divided into cloves.

Then, two seasons later, he dug up a bumper crop and went on to plant an acre of the labor-intensive bulbs. He knew the challenges: plant a garlic clove at high altitude (6,500 feet) in the desert in the fall and hope to get a bulb of 10 to 15 cloves in nine months. Then, reserve a whopping 10 to 12 percent of your crop to plant the next season (instead of the traditional one to two percent required for other crops). Add to that the fact that garlic has a short shelf life, only about six months before it turns hollow on the inside and maybe even moldy, and you might wonder why anyone would be crazy enough to try it season after season.

Stan has an answer: Most garlic in American supermarkets is grown in China. In fact, 90 percent of the world's garlic is grown in China and many of his customers complain that it has no flavor or it's dried out. The garlic grown at El Bosque Farms is fresh in late May and June, and customers are delighted.

Some things have made his job easier over the years. Stan's added a cold frame to extend the season, a drip irrigation system and a Kubota L2850 tractor, which pulls horizontal discs that cut just beneath the garlic bulbs and rarely slices through them.

The schedule is straightforward. Plant in late October, when the weather is cool and the roots begin to grow underground. Wait a number of months until the scapes of hard-neck garlic straighten up or the soft-neck varieties flop over (this usually happens around June), and then gather friends and family for the harvest. When it's time, pull the bulbs from the earth and dry them on long boards.

Long before national health food advocacy movements cropped up, Stan and RoseMary were already operating on these basic principles, providing food that is good and good for you, developing symbiotic relationships with consumers, chefs, farmers and other people involved in food in northern New Mexico.

Stan's first book of nonfiction, *Mayordomo: Chronicle of an Acequia in Northern New Mexico*, explores an old and enduring way of life in small New Mexico villages, where community water rights are vital to farmers and growers. The book chronicles Stan's stint as *mayordomo*, or ditch boss. His second nonfiction book, *A Garlic Testament: Seasons on a Small New Mexico Farm*, tells the story of his life as a garlic farmer. He's also been a pivotal farmer at the Santa Fe Farmers' Market, serving first as a board member and later, as president.

In a funny twist of fate, Stan doesn't much like the taste of garlic, at least not in its raw form. He doesn't much care for beets, broccoli, kale or chard either. So while he knows that eating garlic is good for you, he firmly believes that *growing* your own garlic may be even better for you.

First of all, you've done all the work yourself, with absolutely no assistance from corporate behemoths interested only in the bottom line. It's almost an act of protest. And for this reason Stan is happy to pass on growing tips, so that others can work towards self-reliance with their food.

That's why he's still here, at the market, weighing bags, sharing recipes, connecting with the people who take the time to stop and chat. That's why he still faces what he calls "the tyranny of the fields"—the drought, hail, heat and untimely frosts, the fretting over financial matters. By investing in this old, traditional way of living on and working the land, Stan believes he's found an infinitely more rewarding and healthier lifestyle than, say, investing in stocks, real estate or life insurance. Sure, his garlic sells well, and it's been used in Santa Fe restaurants since the beginning of the city's lauded dining scene in the late 1980s. But it's much bigger than that.

With their farm, Stan and RoseMary are part of the web of life, following generations of farmers before them. No matter how much they struggle, they make ends meet. Beyond that, they are able to contribute hundreds of pounds of what they've grown each year to those far needier.

And so, though he came to New Mexico guided by ideas of self-sufficiency and rugged individualism, Stan found instead a community of like-minded individuals, neighbors who together plant fields and celebrate birthdays, anniversaries and other milestones. Customers who keep coming back for garlic, onions, shallots, kale. And a chance to be part of a culinary renaissance that continues today.

FARM TO TABLE

Americans are concerned about the health and safety of their food and the Farm to Table Movement is just one expression of the disquiet. Proponents—including Alice Waters of Chez Panisse restaurant in Berkeley, author Wendell Berry and food writer Michael Pollan—advocate self-reliance, food security, sustainability and the establishment of a local food system that connects farmers with grocers, chefs, consumers and other stakeholders in the food system.

Across the country, chefs routinely shop their local farmers' markets, in search of fresh, seasonal, locally grown ingredients for that night's menu. Some growers even deliver their fare straight to the restaurant's doorstep. Families shop the markets for healthy food to use throughout the week as well as for the children's activities, live music, baked goods and fresh roasted coffee. Vendors offer cooking demos and share family recipes and cooking techniques.

From coast to coast, the farmers' market has become more than just a place to buy food. It's the heart of many communities, a fabric woven together by the need for sustenance that isn't just filling, but that fills the heart. And, it's at the core of the Farm to Table philosophy—building a community that's interconnected, mutually beneficial and dedicated to providing healthy foods for all.

The farmers' market also represents a living link to the early native people across the continent who grew and ate the very same foods that we eat today—corn, beans, squash, fruits, vegetables, nuts, seeds, beef, turkey and more. Thus, we've come full circle, rediscovering and returning to ancient ways and foods that truly are natural, healthy and delicious.

ROASTED GARLIC

Delicious spread on a French baguette, served with roasted red peppers or tossed with pasta. All you need to know for this recipe is that for each head of garlic, you will need 1 teaspoon of olive oil. Make as much as you like!

Fresh garlic bulbs
Olive oil

Preheat oven to 400 degrees.

Using a sharp knife, slice the tips off the garlic heads, exposing all the cloves inside. Place the bulbs on a baking dish and drizzle each with 1 teaspoon olive oil. Cover with foil and roast until the garlic is soft and it's easy to squeeze out the cloves, about 45 minutes. Serve immediately.

DIXON GARLIC AND WILD MUSHROOMS

SERVES 4

This earthy combination of fresh garlic and wild mushrooms is intoxicating and works well as an appetizer on toast or tossed with pasta as a main dish.

2-3 tablespoons olive oil

5 cloves garlic, sliced

2 cups mushrooms, a combination of shitake, porcini, oyster or
    other wild mushrooms, thickly sliced

¼ cup flat leaf parsley, chopped

¼ teaspoon salt

¼ teaspoon freshly ground black pepper

Heat the oil over medium heat in a large pan. Add the garlic and cook for about a minute. Add the mushrooms and cook, stirring often, until soft and fragrant, about 10 minutes. Add the parsley, season with salt and pepper, and serve hot.

ROASTED SHALLOTS AND FENNEL WITH HARICOTS VERTS

SERVES 4

This flavorful dish combines the sweetness of shallots with the licorice notes of fennel and it pairs well with meat dishes like roast tenderloin, beef ragout and juniper-marinated venison.

¾ cup shallots, peeled, and sliced in half
2 fennel bulbs, trimmed and cut into thin slices
2 tablespoons olive oil
¼ teaspoon salt
¼ teaspoon freshly ground black pepper
1 pound haricots verts (French green beans), ends trimmed

Preheat oven to 375 degrees.

Combine the shallots, fennel, olive oil, salt and pepper in a medium bowl. Place on a baking sheet and roast for 30 minutes, stirring every 10 minutes to ensure even cooking.

Place the beans in salted boiling water and cook for 2 minutes, so they still have a crunch. Drain with cold water.

When the shallots and fennel are done, heat the olive oil in a large sauté pan over medium heat and stir in all the vegetables. Cook for about 5 minutes and serve.

ANGEL HAIR PASTA WITH GARLIC

SERVES 4

This is a very simple dish with complex flavors. The combination of raisins and piñon nuts with garlic, aromatic spices and sharp Parmesan cheese makes a delicious and light meal any time of year.

8 ounces angel hair pasta

1/3 cup olive oil

3 cloves of garlic, sliced

¼ teaspoon red pepper flakes, or to taste

¼ cup fresh parsley, roughly chopped

2 tablespoons of a combination of fresh rosemary, thyme and oregano,
    finely chopped

¼ teaspoon salt

¼ teaspoon freshly ground black pepper

½ cup grated Parmesan cheese plus more for garnish

¼ cup raisins

¼ cup piñon nuts, lightly toasted in pan

Bring salted water to a boil in a large pot and cook the pasta al dente. Drain and rinse and set aside.

Heat olive oil in a small saucepan over medium heat. Add the garlic, red pepper flakes, parsley and other herbs, and cook, stirring constantly, until parsley has wilted, about 1 minute. Remove from heat.

Toss pasta with the herbed garlic sauce in a large bowl. Season with salt and pepper, and stir in the Parmesan cheese, raisins and toasted piñon nuts. Serve with Parmesan cheese.

ACKNOWLEDGMENTS

I am endlessly grateful to the amazing team that helped bring *The Maverick Cookbook* to fruition. Andy Dudzik and Sarah Stark of *Leaf Storm Press* signed on to this project with enthusiasm and provided brilliant inspiration. *And We Ate* of Lambertville, N.J. breathed life into the book with Guy Ambrosino's gorgeous, mouth-watering food photographs and Kate Winslow's culinary expertise with the recipes. Also thanks to Deborah Madison for expertly editing the recipes and to Santa Fe cooking instructor Kathryn Huestler for the very best pie crust recipe.

I'm also grateful to Stanley Crawford and to Priscilla Hoback, daughter of Rosalea Murphy, for their input. And thanks to photographers Don Usner and Doug Magnus for the use of their wonderful photos.

I'm also very grateful to my dad, Tony Cline, my stepmother, Hilary Hays, my brother, Hugh Cline, and my friend, Zia Cross, for reading draft chapters and for making helpful suggestions.

The Maverick Cookbook could never have been written without all the wonderful research that went into its predecessors, especially Huntley Dent's comprehensive *The Feast of Santa Fe* and the many other insightful books about New Mexico cuisine.

Last, but never least, I couldn't have completed this project without the unwavering patience, humor and love provided by my husband and my best friend, Kyle Langan.

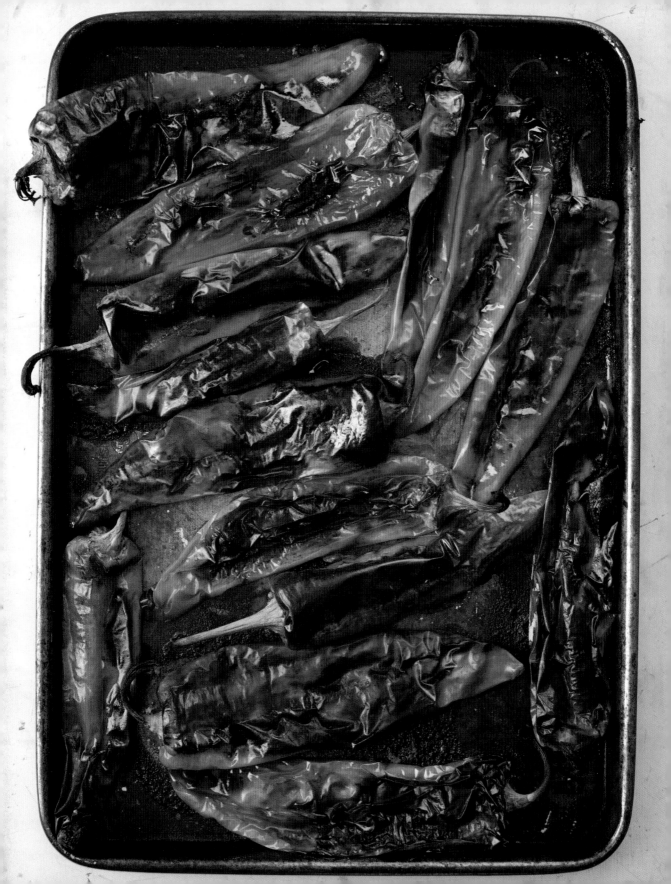

BIBLIOGRAPHY

Arnold, Sam'l P. *Eating Up the Santa Fe Trail: Recipes and Lore From The Old West*. Golden: Fulcrum Publishing, 2001.

Bandelier, Adolf F. *The Delight-Makers*. New York: Dodd, Mead & Company, 1890.

Brown, Patricia Leigh. *The Muse of Taos, Stirring Still*. The New York Times, Jan. 16, 1997.

Church, Peggy Pond. *The House at Otowi Bridge: The Story of Edith Warner and Los Alamos*. Albuquerque: University of New Mexico Press, 1959.

Clark, Marian. *The Route 66 Cookbook: Comfort Food from the Mother Road*. San Francisco/Tulsa: Council Oak Books, 2000.

Cline, Lynn. *Literary Pilgrims: The Santa Fe and Taos Writer's Colonies, 1917-1950*. Albuquerque: University of New Mexico Press, Albuquerque, New Mexico, 2007.

Crawford, Stanley. *A Garlic Testament: Seasons on a Small New Mexico Farm*. Albuquerque: University of New Mexico Press, 1992.

Dent, Huntley. *The Feast of Santa Fe: Cooking of the American Southwest*. New York: Simon & Schuster, 1985.

Fergusson, Erna. *Mexican Cookbook*. Albuquerque: University of New Mexico Press, 1973.

Fried, Stephen. *Appetite for America: Fred Harvey and the Business of Civilizing the Wild West—One Meal at a Time*. New York: Random House, 2011.

Gustave Baumann Property; Historic Architecture Project. Historic Santa Fe Foundation Bulletin, 2009.

Hopper, Marin. "Destiny in Taos," *New York Times, T Magazine*, Sept. 9, 2014.

Jaramillo, Cleofas, **M**. *The Genuine New Mexico Tasty Recipes*. Santa Fe: Ancient City Press, 1981.

Laughlin, Ruth. *The Wind Leaves No Shadow*. Caldwell: Caxton Press, 1948.

Luhan, Mabel Dodge. *Winter in Taos*. Santa Fe: Sunstone Press, 2007.

Magoffin, Susan Shelby. *Down the Santa Fe Trail and into Mexico: The Diary of Susan Shelby Magoffin 1846-1847*. Lincoln: University of Nebraska Press, 1982 (1926).

Murphy, Rosalea. *In the Pink: Southwestern Menus From the World-Famous Pink Adobe Restaurant*. New York; Doubleday, 1993.

Murphy, Rosalea. *The Pink Adobe Cookbook*. New York: Dell Publishing, 1988.

Nesbit, TaraShea. *The Wives of Los Alamos*. New York: Bloomsbury, 2014.

O'Keeffe, Georgia. *Georgia O'Keeffe: A Studio Book*. New York: The Viking Press, 1976.

Robertson, Edna and Nestor, Sarah. *Artists of the Canyons and Caminos: Santa Fe, The Early Years.* Santa Fe: Ancient City Press, 1976.

Rudnick, Lois Palken. *Mabel Dodge Luhan: New Woman, New Worlds.* Albuquerque: University of New Mexico Press, 1984.

Rudnick, Lois Palken. *Utopian Vistas: The Mabel Dodge Luhan House and the American Counterculture.* Albuquerque: University of New Mexico Press, 1996.

Wallis, Michael: *Billy The Kid: The Endless Ride.* New York: W.W. Norton & Co., 2007.

Waters, Frank. *The Woman at Otowi Crossing.* Athens: Swallow Press, 1966.

Weigle, Marta and Fiore, Kyle. *Santa Fe & Taos: The Writer's Era: 1916-1941.* Santa Fe: Ancient City Press, 1994.

Winkler, Peter L. *Dennis Hopper: The Wild Ride of a Hollywood Rebel.* Fort Lee: Barricade Books, 2011.

Wood, Margaret. *A Painter's Kitchen: Recipes from the Kitchen of Georgia O'Keeffe.* Santa Fe: Red Crane Books, 1991.

PHOTO CREDITS

INDEX OF RECIPES

Page numbers in italics refer to photographs.

CONDIMENTS, SAUCES AND EXTRAS

DESSERTS

LUNCH AND DINNER ENTREES

ABOUT THE AUTHOR

Lynn Cline is the author of *Literary Pilgrims: The Santa Fe and Taos Writers' Colonies, 1917-1950* and *Romantic Days and Nights in Santa Fe.* She's also a food writer and blogger and a freelance writer whose work has appeared in *The New York Times, Bon Appetit* and many other publications. She was born in Sweden, grew up in Princeton, New Jersey and lives in Santa Fe, New Mexico with her husband, Kyle.

ABOUT THE PHOTOGRAPHER AND FOOD STYLIST

Guy Ambrosino and Kate Winslow are the husband and wife team behind *And We Ate,* a photography and food styling studio based in Lambertville, New Jersey. But their hearts and sensibilities belong to Santa Fe, where they lived for many years.

Published by Leaf Storm Press
Post Office Box 4670
Santa Fe, New Mexico 87502
LeafStormPress.com

Leaf Storm Press books are available for
special promotions and premiums.
For information, please email
publisher@leafstormpress.com.

ISBN 978-0-9914105-7-6
Library of Congress Control Number: 2015933777

First Edition
Book Design by Alan Hebel and Ian Shimkoviak
Printed in Singapore

10   9   8   7   6   5   4   3   2

Publisher's Cataloging-in-Publication Data
(Provided by Quality Books, Inc.)

Cline, Lynn.
The maverick cookbook : iconic recipes & tales from
New Mexico / by Lynn Cline ; recipe photographs by Guy
Ambrosino. -- First edition.
    pages cm
Includes bibliographical references and index.
    LCCN 2015933777
    ISBN 978-0-9914105-7-6

1. Cooking, American--Southwestern style. 2. Cooking
--New Mexico. 3. New Mexico--History. 4. Cookbooks.
I. Ambrosino, Guy, photographer. II. Title.

TX715.2.S69C556 2015   641.59789
                                  QBI15-600046